"You Can't Air That"

Television and Popular Culture / Robert J. Thompson, *Series Editor*

Other titles in Television and Popular Culture

"Deny All Knowledge": Reading the X Files
David Lavery, Angela Hague, and Marla Cartwright, eds.

Dictionary of Teleliteracy: Television's 500 Biggest Hits, Misses, and Events
David Bianculli

The Gatekeeper: My 30 Years as a TV Censor
Alfred R. Schneider, with Kaye Pullen

*Laughs, Luck . . . and Lucy: How I Came to Create the Most
Popular Sitcom of All Time*
Jess Oppenheimer, with Gregg Oppenheimer

Prime Time, Prime Movers: From I Love Lucy *to* L.A. Law,
America's Greatest TV Shows and the People Who Created Them
David Marc and Robert J. Thompson

Rod Serling's Night Gallery: *An After-Hours Tour*
Scott Skelton and Jim Benson

Storytellers to the Nation: A History of American Television Writing
Tom Stempel

Television's Second Golden Age: From Hill Street Blues *to* ER
Robert J. Thompson

TV Creators: Conversations with America's Top Producers of Television Drama
James L. Longworth, Jr.

Watching TV: Six Decades of American Television, Second Edition
Harry Castleman and Walter Podrazik

"You Can't Air That"

Four Cases

of Controversy

and Censorship

in American Television

Programming

David S. Silverman

 SYRACUSE UNIVERSITY PRESS

Permission to reprint the following lyrics or poetry in chapter 2 is kindly acknowledged: (1) "Waist Deep in the Big Muddy" (The Big Muddy), words and music by Pete Seeger, copyright © 1967 (renewed) Melody Trails, Inc., New York, N.Y.; (2) "The Censor," by Mason Williams, copyright © Mason Williams.

The paper used in this publication meets the minimum requirements of American National Standard of Information Sciences—Permanence of Paper of Printed Library Materials, ANSI Z39.48–1984∞™

For a listing of books published and distributed by Syracuse University Press, visit our Web site at SyracuseUniversityPress.syr.edu

ISBN-13: 978-0-8156-3150-7   ISBN-10: 0-8156-3150-2

Library of Congress Cataloging-in-Publication Data

Silverman, David S.

   You can't air that : four cases of controversy and censorship in American television programming / David S. Silverman.

      p. cm. — (Television and popular culture)

   Includes bibliographical references and index.

   ISBN 978-0-8156-3150-7 (hardcover : alk. paper)

   1. Television programs—United States. 2. Television—Censorship—United States. I. Title.

PN1992.3.U5S555 2007

791.45'75—dc22   2007021383

To Olga and Stephanie, with all of my love

David S. Silverman joined the faculty at Xavier University in New Orleans in fall 2004, where he taught until Hurricane Katrina forced his family to evacuate. He is currently on the faculty of Valley City State University, Valley City, North Dakota, where he teaches a variety of communications and writing courses. Before completing his Ph.D. at the University of Missouri–Columbia, he pursued a six-year career in technical writing for various software and telecommunications companies in Denver, Colorado.

Contents

Acknowledgments

First and foremost, my most profound thanks to and adulation for my wife, Olga, for her encouragement, help, and good sense. Without you, methinks I would go mad.

Special thanks goes to my father, Evan Silverman, for his support over the years. I know that this is a strange business, but it's where I belong. Special thanks also to my mother, Judi Schoendorf, for her support over the years as well. I know that I don't always do things right, but I do strive to do the right things.

Additional thanks goes to:

Dr. William Woodson, the former graduate chair in English at Illinois State University, who inspired me during my master's program to someday become "a Hollywood mogul." Though not one yet, I do study them.

Two late great English teachers, Roberta Reed and Cynthia Beasley, who encouraged my writing in middle school and high school, respectively. Thanks for always believing in me.

Dr. Robert J. Thompson of Syracuse University for his help in bringing this manuscript to publication, and for all of the long telephone conversations about obscure television programs. Also, Ellen Goodman at Syracuse University Press for her patience, persistence, and generosity in extending my deadlines.

Dr. Michael J. Porter of the University of Missouri, my dissertation adviser, for his encouragement and help over the years. You've set a very high bar for me to reach for, and with some hope and some help, I might get there one day.

Dr. Bettina Drew, also of the University of Missouri, a great scholar, good friend, and witness at my wedding, who inspired me to stick with history.

My fellow graduate students, who provided a sounding board for my ideas. I hope that you finally understand what a struggle we've all been through.

Dr. Maria A. Dixon of Southern Methodist University, for "rounding up the troops" in the wake of Hurricane Katrina—your efforts meant a lot to myself and Olga.

Tom DeMoulin of Arapahoe Community College, for helping to recover this manuscript from an Apple-formatted Zip disk that survived its cross-country exodus from Hurricane Katrina.

And finally all of my students, both past and present. You are the future, and I hope that you continue to learn throughout your lives.

"You Can't Air That"

1 Television Censorship and Regulation

An Introduction

Most television producers are more concerned with creating profitable television programs than with creating groundbreaking television; however, some producers, either by accident or by design, create television shows that become part of our cultural legacy. It is also possible, from time to time, for history and profit to be made simultaneously. Programs such as *All in the Family,* the miniseries *Roots,* and *Saturday Night Live* have all been critical, financial, and historical "hits." Many programs, however, are doomed to the darker metaphorical corners of our televised culture. Some shows have had their histories muddied by those individuals with the power to do so, because either their producers or performers "rocked the boat" or a program did not live up to its critical and, more important, financial potential. Further, a select number of these programs either were or became too controversial for their respective networks to continue airing at all.

The clouded histories of such programs, though, push "historians toward a closer engagement with mass communication texts and processes as primary evidence in historical research" through rediscovery and reexamination of such texts (Lipsitz 1988, 149). Such an examination of television programming as text should also be coupled with an understanding of the sociopolitical forces that helped to shape their production in the first place, as well as an understanding of how popular artists produce messages for mass audiences. Another factor to consider about the production of television programming is the realization that there is a group that stands between the popular artist and his or her audience. To the public, this group consists of faceless individuals: the producers, the sponsors, and the networks' "Standards and Practices Departments": "They are powerful, for they exert controls over the popular artist and the artifact. Their success depends in no small way on their ability to read the pulse of mass society, to feel the same things as mass society feels, to enlarge the audience, or to create a new audience that previously did not exist" (Dunlop 1975, 378). At the same time, each network's Standards and Practices Department, commonly known as "censors," acts as the network's penultimate guardian and arbiter of its image (the ultimate being the network's president). Censors read scripts, attend every part of the production process, and often preview programs before they are aired. If a program fails to conform to a network's standards, even if they seem arbitrary, the censor can insist on changes. If a program producer fails to comply with the requests of the censor, the program probably will not air. This book examines the historical contexts, content, and controversies surrounding the production of four television programs that aired on the four major broadcast networks between the years 1967 and 2002.

This book also focuses on what has been seen as an often reactionary (and preemptory) type of censorship—corporate censorship—a form of censorship that all four programs experienced while they aired at their respective television networks. As you read, remember that corporate censorship has been shaped by different Federal Communications Commission (FCC) mandates, court rulings,[1] and laws since broadcasting began and should

---

1. Specifically, *Miller v. California* in 1973 and *FCC v. Pacifica Foundation* in

not to be confused with governmental censorship. Although the First Amendment guards against governmental interference with "the press" and the FCC is specifically prohibited from preemptory censorship of broadcasts, First Amendment protections do not directly apply with regards to radio or television, owing to the government's role in licensing all broadcast stations. These licenses are issued for and held accountable to the public good or, more specifically, ill-defined community standards—a constantly changing and highly variable target.[2] The FCC involves itself with broadcast material only after a given broadcast if there are sufficient complaints that a broadcast has violated those standards. If the FCC determines that a broadcast contained indecent material, then and only then can the FCC levy fines or revoke broadcast licenses. It is this dangling "sword of Damocles," if you will, that has frightened broadcasters, until only very recently, away from broadcasting material that may violate a community's standards—resulting in the charge that networks have traditionally played to the lowest common denominator by broadcasting bland and inoffensive programming.

In order to better understand the forces that shaped commercial network television in the United States in the last half of the

---

1978. *Miller* was concerned with broadcasting obscene materials, which led Justice Potter Stewart to observe, "I know it when I see it." *Pacifica* created a distinction between obscene and indecent material, the former of which was prohibited under *Miller*, determining the latter to be protected speech—but only when children are not likely to be watching.

2. It should also be noted that the FCC—as of the printing of this text—does not have any regulatory control over cable networks because they are not "broadcast" over the public airwaves and because cable television is available only as a subscription service and therefore is subject to the First Amendment. Cable operators, fearful of any more governmental interference, choose to broadcast their riskier material when children are not as likely to be watching—hence, Cinemax broadcasts soft-core adult films around midnight, leading to its nickname, "Skinemax."

twentieth century, a background history of the regulatory forces (governmental, commercial, and pressure group) is presented. It is my intent to show how these regulatory forces, and the pressures they bear on commercial network television in the United States, have historically shaped the way that television networks monitor and self-censor what is (or is not) seen by the American public.

A Brief History of Television (Self-)Regulation

The Commission on Freedom of the Press:
A Warning at the Birth of Television

In 1942, Henry Luce Jr., the publisher of *Time,* provided two hundred thousand dollars, while *Encyclopaedia Britannica* provided fifteen thousand dollars, to fund the independent Commission on Freedom of the Press (CFP). The commission's published findings, *A Free and Responsible Press,* were presented at the dawn of postwar television in 1947. The group became known as the Hutchins Commission for its head, Robert Hutchins of the University of Chicago. The CFP was "composed of nine professors, one businessman, two presidents of institutions of higher learning, and a man of letters who had served as an assistant secretary of state" (Leab 1970, 106). The CFP defined "the press" to "include within its scope the major agencies of mass communication: the radio, newspapers, motion pictures, magazines, and books" (The Commission on Freedom of the Press 1947, v). During its four-year investigation, the CFP took testimony from 58 men and women who worked for the press as well as 225 members of private agencies, companies, and government officials who dealt with the press. Although the commission examined how mass communication agencies worked to educate the public, the commission was convinced that American culture was affected by the creators of mass communication.

The Hutchins Commission's view of mass communication was not single-minded, noting that the media were not the only influences on American culture or public opinion; however, the commission acknowledged that it most likely was the most powerful influence in American society. In its conclusion in 1947—which is easily true of American society today—the commission claimed that "contemporary life is a terrifying flood of words with which the agencies of mass communication threaten to inundate the citizen" (vii–viii). The commission also warned the American public that if anyone had nothing critical or controversial to say about society, such inoffensive material could easily be released with "a knowing press agent, or a considerable reputation, or an active pressure group . . . whereas, even with such advantages, anybody with something to say has a hard time getting it said by mass communication if it runs counter to the ideas of owners, editors, opposing pressure groups, or popular prejudice" (viii). Thus, the CFP found that whereas the "doctrine that the freedom of the press gives to the agencies of mass communication, as a matter of right, to those who have nothing to say . . . the tremendous influence of the modern press makes it imperative that the great agencies of mass communication show hospitality to ideas which their owners do not share" (viii). In short, the commission concluded that the greatest threat to free and open debate of controversial topics lies in the hands of the owners of mass communication outlets; however, the report concluded that short of governmental interference or enforcement to ensure a free and open press, self-regulation could be effective if performed earnestly.

At the time the CFP met, television's progress had been halted by World War II. By the time the CFP published its findings on mass communication in 1947, history revealed its shortsightedness in ignoring television as a mass medium: 3.9 million people watched the 1947 World Series on television, the medium's first mass audience. By 1948, network television, though still in its infancy, saw the birth of several long-running series, and by 1949,

Chicago and New York were linked by cable, with the West Coast linked in 1951. As the major players of early television were the already established radio networks—principally, the National Broadcasting Company (NBC), Columbia Broadcasting System (CBS), and American Broadcasting Companies (ABC)—and regulation of broadcast television came under the auspices of the FCC, the National Association of Broadcasters (NAB) also applied its voluntary code to its members who ventured into the new medium. These voluntary codes, established by and for the member stations of the NAB, coupled with the influence of advertisers, established the self-regulatory content controls for television until the early 1960s.

Regulating Radio with Pictures: The NAB Steps In

The NAB was founded by the radio industry in 1923 and initially attempted to self-regulate the industry until the 1926 radio-wavelength wars. When this self-regulation failed, the federal government stepped in—first with the Radio Act of 1927, and then with the Communications Act of 1934, the latter of which led to the creation of the FCC. Despite its age and its subsequent numerous amendments, the Communications Act of 1934 still provides the principal legal authority for the FCC's power to regulate the public airwaves. However, as Gary W. Selnow and Richard R. Gilbert point out, the FCC's role is still strictly limited, as "Section 326 of the Communications Act expressly forbids the FCC to censor broadcast material" (1993, 87). The Hutchins Commission noted in 1947 that the NAB had "no machinery for the censorship of programs" (1947, 72) and that joining the NAB and conforming to its code were strictly voluntary. The commission further noted that whereas the Communications Act of 1934 protected radio from censorship, advertisers protected radio from controversy (and boycotts) through strong control of content. This kind of content control would later shape the NAB Television Code of 1952.

The NAB Television Code of 1952

The NAB Television Code of 1952 retained much of the radio code, urging broadcasters to air sufficient amounts of educational and cultural programming, and contained only a few "prohibitions, but its underlying premise seemed to be that critics were more concerned about what was not being broadcast than about what was being broadcast" (MacCarthy 1995, 672). However, the new television code did contain an enforcement mechanism, creating a television-code review board to listen to complaints. NAB subscribers who voluntarily submitted to the code would obtain a code seal for respecting the content restrictions and were subject to penalties established by the review board. These restrictions included:

> Interdictions on profanity and obscenity, any words derisive of any race, color, creed, etc., any attacks on religion. On the positive side there are pointers that respect be maintained for the sanctity of marriage and the value of the home. Illicit sex relations are not to be treated as commendable. Narcotics addiction should not be represented except as vicious habit, and . . . the detailed presentation of brutality or physical agony by sight or by sound are not permissible. (Hoyt and Hoyt 1970, 45)

Ironically, the American Civil Liberties Union attacked the new television code amid fears that it was illegally suppressing freedom of expression and asked the FCC to determine if "the code violated the provisions of the Communications Act banning censorship" (MacCarthy 1995, 675).

Politics and Public Pressure: The Red Scare Hits the Small Screen

Another force shaping the television landscape in the late 1940s and early 1950s was a bit more geopolitical. From the start of the cold war, members of the House Un-American Activities Committee

(HUAC), as well as Senator Joseph McCarthy, made it their duty to rid the United States of Communists, real or imagined. Aiding them in this "struggle" were the anti-Communist work *Counterattack*, published by American Business Consultants, as well as the book *Red Channels: The Report of Communist Influence in Radio and Television*. The latter, published in 1950, was based in part on the HUAC hearings and "listed 151 people—alphabetically arranged for easy reference—with 'citations'" and included "the most talented and admired people in the [show business] industry—mostly writers, directors, and performers" (Barnouw 1990, 122). Eric Barnouw describes some of the "citations" that merited being blacklisted in *Red Channels:* "They had opposed Franco, Hitler, and Mussolini, tried to help war refugees, combated race discrimination, campaigned against poll taxes and other voting barriers, opposed censorship, criticized the House committee on un-American activities, hoped for peace, and favored efforts toward better U.S.-Soviet relations. Most had been New Deal supporters" (124).[3] Within days of the publication of *Red Channels*, the Korean War broke out, and worried television broadcasting executives looked at the list against the backdrop of the war against Communism. Fearing the loss of its prized advertisers, the television (and film) industry began to quietly use the list in hiring decisions.[4]

A Supermarket Crusader

Concurrent with the appearance of *Red Channels* and *Counterattack* was the emergence of the seemingly grassroots anti-Communist

---

3. For further descriptions of the blacklist and McCarthyism, I suggest Alvie Bessie's *Inquisition in Eden* (East Berlin: Seven Seas Publishers, 1965); Victor S. Navasky's *Naming Names* (New York: Penguin Books, 1981); and actor Robert Vaughn's published dissertation *Only Victims* (New York: G. P. Putnam's Sons, 1972).

4. Interestingly, Broadway producers ignored the list, and many blacklisted performers found regular work there, including Burgess Meredith and Zero Mostel.

effort of "supermarket crusader" Eleanor Johnson Buchanan. Buchanan began the supermarket crusade after her husband was sent to Korea, but her efforts alone held little sway. However, her father, Laurence A. Johnson, who owned four grocery stores in Syracuse, New York, had been recently elected to office in the National Association of Supermarkets. This position gave Johnson the illusion of great power over the supermarket industry, power that he used to pressure the sponsors of television programs that were using blacklisted performers, such as *Danger*, an early CBS drama, and *The Name's the Same*, an ABC game program produced by Mark Goodson.[5]

According to veteran game-show producer Mark Goodson (1991), writer Abe Burrows—whose credits included the Broadway hit *Guys and Dolls*—was hounded off *The Name's the Same* by Johnson, whose tactic was to threaten the sponsor of any program who hired "subversives" by hanging signs over its products on store shelves. In the case of *The Name's the Same*, Swanson Frozen Foods felt the heat in the form of a ballot Johnson passed out to customers that read, "Do you want any part of your purchase price of Swanson Foods to be used to hire Communist fronters? Indicate your choice by x in the appropriate box" (Goodson 1991, 40). With the threat that such a ballot would be distributed to grocery stores nationwide, Swanson Frozen Foods forced Goodson to fire Burrows from the program. Testimonials for Johnson's crusade poured in from other companies, such as Kraft Foods and the General Ice Cream Corporation, who wrote to him, "I think it is wonderful that you have taken this interest in ferreting communists out of the entertainment industry" (Barnouw 1990, 127).

5. Mark Goodson's personal account of those dark days was titled "If I'd Stood Up Earlier" (1991).

Using the Instrument to Illuminate:
Edward R. Murrow Takes on McCarthyism

Meanwhile, at CBS, Edward R. Murrow and Fred Friendly had created the first televised newsmagazine, *See It Now,* in 1951.[6] Murrow was one of the most recognized and esteemed broadcasters in the United States, best known to American audiences for his rooftop broadcasts from London during the blitz of World War II. By 1953, his program had become one of the most influential news programs on the air, and Murrow wanted to weigh in on the growing anti-Communist mania that was sweeping the United States. Friendly states that he encouraged Murrow not to directly attack McCarthy himself—which, objectivity aside, was Murrow's ultimate goal—but to find a small story that had national significance. Murrow found it in the form of Milo Radulovich, a U.S. Air Force weatherman who had been labeled a security risk because his father and sister allegedly read Communist-sympathetic newspapers. CBS, afraid of an anti-Communist backlash, refused to provide any promotional spots for the program, so Murrow and Friendly paid for advertising out of their own pockets. Once the program had aired, the secretary of the air force examined the case and reinstated Radulovich's commission. The Radulovich broadcast, which showed television's power to influence public policy, marked the beginning of the end for Murrow at CBS.

In the aftermath of the Radulovich broadcast, Joseph Wershba, one of Murrow's producers, was approached by Don Surine, McCarthy's chief investigator (Wershba 2000). The conversation that followed detailed a direct threat to Murrow from the junior senator from Wisconsin: Surine had found that in 1934, Murrow had

6. For a full account of *See It Now,* see Fred Friendly's account of the program in his text *Due to Circumstances Beyond Our Control . . .* (New York: Vintage, 1967).

worked for the Institute of International Education, which sponsored a summer exchange of American and Soviet scholars that year. Surine, using McCarthyesque logic, hinted that this background meant that Murrow, therefore, had been on the Soviet payroll, because the Soviets had provided some funding for the exchange program. Surine went on to threaten (again indirectly) Murrow's brother, an air force general.

The threat of becoming a McCarthy target placed Murrow in a difficult situation: at the time, McCarthy was still at the top of his game, but the threat could not be ignored. Friendly began assembling a collection of McCarthy news clips for a program that would show the senator's most controversial—and often contradictory—statements. Then Murrow and Friendly waited until the senator himself became vulnerable. In February 1954, their moment came. McCarthy openly attacked the U.S. Army for harboring Communists, which culminated in what has become known as the Army-McCarthy hearings. Although these televised hearings began to pierce the McCarthy machine, Murrow's *See It Now* would help finish the job. Knowing this likelihood, Friendly revealed the content of the March 9, 1954, program to William Paley, the owner of CBS, with only a few days' notice. The CBS reaction was similar to the Radulovich broadcast: the network would not provide any advance promotion of the McCarthy show.

Murrow and Friendly had, with the precision of journalists at the top of their craft, created a treatise that revealed the dark, twisted nature of Senator McCarthy to a nation that had begun to grow weary of the rants of the aimless (and eponymous) political witch hunt that is his legacy. McCarthy's rebuttal, a requirement of the Fairness Doctrine, that Murrow was on the Soviet payroll, was just as aimless in the face of Murrow's carefully crafted arguments and was easily dismissed by the viewing public as just another overreach.

Between the *See It Now* broadcasts, the Army-McCarthy hearings, and growing public sentiment, McCarthy soon found himself censured by the U.S. Senate. Curiously, despite the success that Murrow had achieved in helping to craft that public sentiment, Murrow himself faced censure from CBS. Paley did not like the fact that Murrow had used Paley's network to wield such a strong editorial against McCarthy, and Murrow would now pay the price for his insolence. His reward for helping to end McCarthyism was to see his program reduced to a series of specials, his editorial voice diminished, and the forced breakup of his partnership with Friendly once *See It Now* was canceled in 1958.

Enforcing the Blacklist: Standards and Practices Departments Take Over

Each network, advertising agency, and sponsor in turn exchanged information on a regular basis about blacklisted performers and artists and employed security people to clear performers who were to be on the air. If an individual appeared on "the list," he or she was not used, but nor were such tactics revealed to the affected performers—they were simply labeled "bad actors" or given any other number of brush-offs. As the networks battled to keep their sponsors happy by keeping their programs stocked with "cleared" performers, they quietly codified the use of blacklists to avoid the appearance of supporting Communism. Sponsors were also pressured by the threat of massive boycotts and bad publicity from the likes of the Syracuse supermarket crusader. For the remainder of the 1950s, advertisers would remain firmly in control of all content on the programs they sponsored until the quiz-show scandal of the late 1950s, when it was revealed during a congressional hearing that certain contestants were either given the answers before a broadcast or quietly paid to lose on air.

Fearing public outrage and government-mandated controls following the quiz-show scandal, the networks reassumed operational control of their programs. This approach meant that the networks, not the advertisers, had direct editorial responsibility for what was ultimately aired. For programming that was not directly created by a network, independent producers had to follow that network's "standards and practices," and although advertisers were kept directly out of the loop, they could still use their financial power to influence programming content.[7] The networks also strengthened their Standards and Practices Departments to guard themselves from the perception of corruption and controversy.[8]

A Maturing Medium: Television Censorship and Regulation in the 1960s and 1970s

Although the dawn of the 1960s saw less emphasis on the Communist blacklist, strict adherence to the NAB code was the mantra of the (then) Big Three networks, as network programming departments remained fearful of producing controversial or explosive material. Much of the networks' offerings during this time were trouble free and squeaky clean (and, more important, advertiser friendly!), as programs such as *The Adventures of Ozzie & Harriet, Petticoat Junction,* and *Bonanza* filled much of the networks' slates. The early sixties saw some controversy over the amount of violence in network programming, with much of the debate focused on one program, *The Untouchables,* whereas other cop shows (such as *The Naked City*), westerns (*Cheyenne, Gunsmoke,* and *The Outlaws*), and

7. Perhaps the most notorious example was the American Gas Association's sponsorship of Playhouse 90's *Judgment at Nuremburg.* At their insistence, all reference to gas—including "gas chambers"—was omitted from the made-for-TV movie. The subsequent Oscar-winning film version of the same play had no such omissions.

8. By 1960, the open hiring of Hollywood Ten screenwriter Dalton Trumbo by both Otto Preminger and Stanley Kubrick helped to break the grip that the blacklist held over Hollywood films, but TV was still steadfast in maintaining the list.

anthology series *(One Step Beyond* and *The Twilight Zone)* drew less criticism over content.

Thomas Dodd and the First Senate Hearings on Televised Violence

Beginning in June 1961, Senator Thomas Dodd, chair of the Senate Subcommittee to Investigate Juvenile Delinquency of the Committee on the Judiciary, convened the first congressional investigation to determine if there was a link between televised violence and the apparent increase of violent crime in the United States. An easy target for Dodd was the nation's network executives for the threefold increase in violence seen in prime-time programming (Schneider with Pullen 2001). By January 1962, Dodd provoked the broadcasters into a First Amendment fight for control of the content seen on network television: "When decisions regarding the major portion of the broadcasts which enter each home are concentrated in the hands of a few men at the head of each network, then we rightly look to their decisions and ask how well the public interest, which broadcasters are under duty to serve under the Federal Communications Act, is being served by a program schedule overloaded with 'crime and violence'" (U.S. Senate 1962, 2406). Senator Dodd understood the implications such a statement could mean, so he tempered it by paraphrasing the late Joseph Klapper as the reason for his concern: "If depictions of crime and violence have an unhealthy effect upon even one percent of the nation's children, it becomes socially important to inquire whether and how the situation can be rectified. . . . we must realize that whatever the medium we attempt to evaluate—be it newspaper, the radio, television, or any other medium, we are dealing with the fundamental question in our democratic society of freedom of speech" (2406).

During the Senate hearings, Oliver Treyz, the president of ABC-TV, was questioned over the content of the premiere episode of *Bus*

Stop that aired on October 1, 1961, featuring the singer Fabian Forte as a delinquent named Luke accused of murder. Though tame by today's standards, the program had prompted a television code report that "indicated the need to edit portrayal of the murder, reduce use of a switchblade knife, and eliminate vulgar language and implied salaciousness in Luke's whisper to a young lady" (Schneider with Pullen 2001, 13). Yet when Dodd asked Treyz if he had allowed his own children to watch the program, Treyz admitted that he had not. Soon after this admission, Treyz lost his job at ABC in order to placate both public outcry and fear of governmental action. Additionally, the NAB quickly acted out of fear of stronger legislation from Washington by incorporating the concerns of the Dodd committee into revisions to the NAB Television Code and Television Code Review Board. The NAB's Television Code Authority office began to monitor violence in programming after a program aired, because all three networks were against prescreening of programs as a form of prior restraint—a topic that would reemerge during the Pastore hearings by the end of the decade.

Censorship of Sex and Violence: The Pastore Investigation

In the first few months of 1969, Senator John Pastore of Rhode Island began exploring ways to reduce televised sex and violence. According to Geoffrey Cowan, the networks would have done well to listen to Senator Pastore's thoughts about regulating the airwaves:

> To broadcasters, Pastore was a uniquely important official. As chairman of the Senate Communications Subcommittee, he presided over all broadcaster-related legislation, and some of the legislation then in front of his committee was worth literally hundreds of millions of dollars to the broadcasting industry. In addition, Senator Pastore's committee had to pass all proposed presidential appointees to the Federal Communications Commission, which is responsible for renewing, or

refusing to renew, all broadcasting licenses. As if that weren't power enough, Pastore also served as chairman of the Senate Appropriations Subcommittee that controlled the FCC's budget. (Cowan 1978, 54)[9]

Senator Pastore was at first concerned about the sexually suggestive material of a Noxema shaving cream commercial, in which a Swedish bombshell seductively tells her shaving companion to "take it off . . . take it all off" (54). Pastore's reaction to this commercial concerned any possible negative effects this commercial might have on his grandchild. Pastore also focused his attention on the political and religious satire that appeared on programs such as *Laugh-In* and *The Smothers Brothers Comedy Hour (TSBCH)*.

Early in 1969, Pastore crafted a plan to keep objectionable material from ever airing, in the form of prescreenings before the NAB Television Code Authority. Pastore also warned broadcasters that if they were unable to self-regulate, he would press for new legislation that would ensure "the security and stability of broadcast licenses . . . to an industry whose members had nightmares that the FCC might not renew their licenses" (55). Pressing the networks to cooperate, Pastore gave them until March 24, 1969—the date he was scheduled to address the NAB—to provide a response, to which ABC and NBC reluctantly agreed, with CBS the lone holdout. In a letter that was hand-delivered to Pastore before his speech, then CBS president Frank Stanton stood up for the First Amendment and the rights of broadcasters to be free of governmental interference:

> The expeditious course for CBS—certainly the more cautious course—would be to accommodate your view and accede to your proposal. I say this out of respect for your position, and

9. Geoffrey Cowan's father, Louis Cowan, was once the president of CBS but was ousted in 1959 during the game-show scandal.

in full knowledge of the many difficulties which the industry presently faces. But in the final analysis, we have decided that we cannot—and in the public interest should not—accede to a proposal which would [make the NAB Television Code Authority] the single final arbiter of network television entertainment that the American people would be permitted to see. . . . [W]ere CBS to share the responsibility for its program decisions with the National Association of Broadcasters, it would only be a matter of time before the government would go to the Code Authority about our performance—initially to inquire, then to urge. This would spell the beginning of the end of our independence. (55–56)

Ironically, within two weeks of taking this stance, the newly installed CBS television network president, Robert Wood, fired the Smothers Brothers for failure to deliver a tape of their Easter program for prescreening. The firing of the Smothers Brothers may have satiated Pastore, and by the conclusion of the hearings in 1969, Senator Pastore did not come forward with his proposed legislation to enforce self-regulation. Instead, Pastore wrote to the secretary of health, education, and welfare to request that he and the surgeon general appoint a committee to determine if there were any effects of television violence on children.

Protecting Children: The Surgeon General's Report of 1972

In the early 1970s, the networks took a sudden interest in their respective children's television-programming content again, this time out of fear of the proposed restrictive guidelines that the FCC was crafting. These new rules were themselves a response, in part, to the conclusions found in *Television and Social Behavior: A Technical Report to the Surgeon General's Scientific Advisory Committee on Television and Social Behavior* (Comstock, Rubinstein, and Murray 1972), the study of television violence that Senator Pastore had suggested. Based on the suggestions found in the surgeon general's study, the FCC crafted a set of guidelines known as "Children's Television Programs: Report and Policy Statement" in 1974. The guidelines required all licensees to make clear separations, known as "bumpers," to delineate programs from commercials, an idea that was incorporated into the NAB code almost immediately. Network executives began to see the writing on the blackboard, so to speak, and, fearing further regulatory filters, individually began their own efforts to self-improve and self-regulate in advance of any further FCC dictates.

Concurrent with the surgeon general's study on the impact of television on children, grassroots efforts and scholarly scrutiny of the impact of television on children began to draw the interest of both elected officials and federal regulators. Responding to the growing criticism of children's television, ABC Television asked the NAB in January 1972 for a reduction in and a modification of commercial airtime during children's weekend television programs. This push by ABC, to phase in a reduction from sixteen minutes of commercials to eleven minutes per hour (or eight minutes to five and a half minutes per half hour), was opposed by CBS, and a twelve-minute compromise was eventually worked out through multilateral negotiations.

By early 1973, Scott Ward, Greg Reale, and David Levinson's landmark 1972 paper, "Children's Perceptions, Explanations, and Judgments of Television Advertising: A Further Exploration," gave ammunition to the grassroots effort opposed to the perceived harm commercial television was inflicting on the nation's children. These groups, such as Action for Children's Television (ACT), in turn used political pressure to prompt further congressional and FCC hearings on the subject of federal regulations and children's television-programming content.

With growing political pressure, the FCC intervened where it had previously relied on self-regulation by the broadcast networks.

In its ruling on children's advertising policy in 1974, the FCC recommended—but did not enforce—limits of nine and a half minutes of ad time on weekends and twelve minutes of ad time on weekdays, which closely mirrored the self-regulatory standards that had been recently adopted by the NAB.

The Family Viewing Hour

Another reaction to the surgeon general's 1972 report, as well as to the growing public and congressional concern, came in the form of the "Family Viewing Hour." The concept was originally proposed to the heads of all three networks in November 1974 by FCC chairman Richard Wiley, who felt pressured, in the form of both punitive action by Congress and bad publicity from groups such as ACT, to do something to protect children from televised violence. As a result of Wiley's proposition, CBS proposed the creation of a two-hour safe haven every evening between the hours of seven and nine o'clock eastern time, in a January 7, 1975, speech to the NAB. Pushed by Arthur Taylor, the newly installed president of CBS, and endorsed—but not mandated—by the FCC, CBS then proposed the Family Viewing Hour as an amendment to the NAB code. Once formally adopted, each network reviewed its schedules and moved its more controversial and violent programming into later time slots.

Reacting to the adoption of the Family Viewing Hour, the Writers Guild of America, Norman Lear (producer of *All in the Family*), Larry Gelbart (producer of *M*A*S*H*), Danny Arnold (producer of *Barney Miller*), and other independent producers challenged the NAB policy in a California federal district court in November 1975, claiming that the new policy infringed on their First Amendment rights and would harm them financially. Their challenge hinged on the role that FCC chairman Wiley had played in the creation of the Family Viewing Hour, as the lawsuit ventured into uncharted legal territory. Meanwhile, the policy, as created by all three television networks and supported by the NAB and the FCC, "had the sound of motherhood" as well as the support of 82 percent of the American public (Cowan 1978, 163).

One year later, Judge Warren Ferguson ventured into that uncharted legal territory. Ferguson determined that when FCC chairman Wiley recommended the Family Viewing Hour policy to the three networks, he had violated both the First Amendment's censorship clause as well as the Administrative Procedure Act, which requires that before taking any formal action, agencies such as the FCC must provide public hearings and encourage public participation. The court reaffirmed the self-regulatory actions of privately held networks but also believed that when the networks and the NAB had acted in collaboration with the FCC, the compromise—the Family Viewing Hour—was given the appearance of a government-authorized mandate. Judge Ferguson ruled, however, that each network could continue the Family Viewing Hour if its decision to do so was based on independent conceptions of what was best for the public good.

Even before the ruling, CBS's ratings had plummeted, and everyone associated with the Family Viewing Hour—including its most staunch cocreator, Arthur Taylor—was either fired or forced to resign. In a surprising twist, the United States Court of Appeals for the Ninth Circuit ruled three years later that the primary jurisdiction for deciding whether the Family Viewing Hour policy was constitutional was the FCC, not the California Federal District Court. The court of appeals vacated the lower court's decision and handed the matter back to the FCC.

Further complicating matters, in a 1982 consent decree, the Justice Department effectively ended the NAB Television Code on the grounds that it violated antitrust issues with regards to advertising standards. A year later, on September 23, 1983, the FCC determined that the networks had crafted and adopted the NAB Family Viewing Hour voluntarily and that former FCC chairman

Wiley had not acted improperly. The lawsuit was settled in May 1984 between the networks and the plaintiffs, casting aside the First Amendment claim of the original suit. Each network finished the deregulation-driven 1980s with an individual Standards and Practices Department, with each network's claim of family viewing more of a promotional slogan than an industrywide promise to create such programming.

The Fast and Loose 1980s: The Great Communicator Deregulates

Federal regulators at the FCC pulled back their controls at the beginning of the Reagan administration, with the impact of such deregulation first felt in children's television in the early 1980s, then with the abandonment of the Fairness Doctrine in 1987. Ronald Reagan's FCC appointee, Mark Fowler, believed that the government should get out of the way with respect to regulating the broadcasting industry, allowing for a marketplace approach instead.

G.I. Joe Is Educational, If You Want to Know How to Buy an Action Figure

Spearheading the Reagan administration's efforts at deregulation across the board, including the deregulation of children's television, Fowler moved to abandon the 1974 FCC rules, which has stated that "the medium of television cannot live up to its potential of serving America's children unless individual broadcasters are genuinely committed to that task, and are willing—to a considerable extent—to put profit in second place and children in first" (Federal Communications Commission 1974, 11). One of the results of this deregulation was that toy makers began animation production companies to skirt both the FCC and the self-regulatory host-selling rules through the creation of toy-driven programs such as *The Transformers, Gobots,* and *G.I. Joe.* As these programs took over, the availability of quality educational programming was reduced to the offerings found on the Public Broadcasting Service (PBS) and cable television. The rest of the 1980s would see public and congressional sentiment change, as the debate over children's television increased, eventually culminating in the passage of the Children's Television Act of 1990.

The Fairness Doctrine: Constitutional but Not Enforced

Similar deregulation occurred with the Fairness Doctrine. The Fairness Doctrine was developed by the FCC over many years and had three specific requirements: that broadcasters cover controversial matters with balance, cover alternative points of view, and provide equal time to any person or organization that is criticized during a broadcast. First set forth in 1941 in the *Mayflower* case, which reinforced the Communications Act's requirement that broadcast licensees act in the public interest, the FCC at first required licensees to cease editorializing. The FCC then reversed itself; instead of eliminating editorials, the FCC determined that licensees could make editorials, so long as they provided equal coverage to all aspects of a given issue. This rule, then, led the commission to require licensees to cover and explore all sides of issues of public importance. This slow evolution of the Fairness Doctrine into the three-pronged version listed above went unchallenged until 1964, when Red Lion Broadcasting fought it on constitutional grounds.[10]

During the election year of 1964, Fred Cook wrote *Goldwater: Extremist on the Right,* a book that criticized Barry Goldwater, the Republican nominee for president. In response to this text, a conservative minister, the Reverend Billy Hargis, criticized the book on a station that Red Lion Broadcasting owned in Philadelphia, accusing Cook of lying and of being a Communist. When Cook

---

10. *Mayflower Broadcasting Corp.,* 8 F.C.C. 333 (1941); *Red Lion Broadcasting v. Federal Communications Commission,* 395 U.S. 367, 89 S.Ct. 1794, 23 L.Ed. 2d 371 (1969).

asked Red Lion for airtime to respond to Hargis's accusations, Red Lion refused, and Cook asked the FCC for relief under the Fairness Doctrine, which then ordered Red Lion to comply. Red Lion appealed the FCC edict in the Washington, D.C., Court of Appeals, claiming that its First Amendment rights were threatened by the FCC's order. When the court of appeals upheld the FCC order, the Supreme Court reviewed the decision and ruled once again in favor of the FCC, on the grounds that because all stations must be licensed in order to avoid overlapping frequencies, such licensing creates a scarcity on the broadcast spectrum, and therefore broadcast licensees must, under the Fairness Doctrine, provide for the public interest by ensuring time for injured parties to respond to attacks.

By 1985, the FCC, under Reagan appointee Mark Fowler, revisited the Fairness Doctrine and, despite the *Red Lion* decision, determined that it was unconstitutional. Specifically, the FCC claimed that the Fairness Doctrine "lessened the amount of diverse views available to the public, inhibited the expression of unorthodox opinions, placed government into the intrusive role of scrutinizing program content, created the opportunity for intimidation of broadcasters by government officials, imposed unnecessary economic costs upon broadcasters and the FCC, and did not protect either broadcasters or the public from undue influence" (Heinke and Tremain 2000, 45). Adding to this opinion was the growth of outlets on cable television, and as the *Red Lion* case was based on scarcity of media outlets, in 1987 the FCC recommended that the Fairness Doctrine be dropped. Congress attempted to legislate the Fairness Doctrine into law in 1987, but Reagan vetoed the bill it was attached to, and all subsequent attempts to reinstate the Fairness Doctrine have failed. However, some believe that as fewer and fewer media conglomerates control all forms of media, the need for the renewal of the Fairness Doctrine is important in protecting the public interest.

The Late 1980s: Networks Cut Back on Their Censors

During this era of deregulation at the FCC and coupled with the loss of the NAB Television Code Authority, the networks also began to trim their budgets through cutbacks in their Standards and Practices Departments. In 1988, with an eye toward the bottom line, both NBC and CBS eliminated their respective standards and practices staffs entirely, and there was a sharp reduction in staff at ABC's Broadcast Standards and Practices Department. At NBC and CBS, other departments became responsible for programs that had yet to air, while the control of objectionable material was left to the program producer and network programmers.

With the NAB Television Code eliminated and the FCC abandoning its role of monitoring content for salacious material—citing First Amendment rights and an increase in the number of program sources—the era of self-regulation with regards to objectionable content ended. This discontinuation led to an increase in grassroots protests, such as the one led by Terry Rakolta of Michigan. Rakolta, presented in the media as a Michigan mother and housewife, became concerned when she tuned into a broadcast of *Married . . . with Children* and decided to take action over what she perceived to be an increase in sleaze. Like the supermarket crusader thirty years before her, Rakolta wrote to the program's advertisers and threatened an economic boycott, a threat that managed to persuade companies such as Kimberly-Clark, McDonald's, and Procter and Gamble to stop their advertising on *Married . . . with Children*. This modest success was short-lived, however. Rakolta's outcry, and the press attention it drew, produced a larger audience for the program, as viewers tuned in to see what all the commotion was about. And where there is a larger audience, other advertisers will follow. *Married . . . with Children* became one of the fledgling Fox Network's longest-running hits, and although Fox executives refused to air one episode because they believed it too racy even for them,[11] the overall content of the program was never altered in response to the threatened boycott and the flight of frightened advertisers.

The 1990s and Beyond

The Children's Television Act of 1990

Responding to public pressure regarding the state of children's television in the deregulated 1980s, Congress passed the Children's Television Act of 1990. The act was designed to limit the number of commercials directed at children, as well as require licensees to serve both the educational and the informational needs of children throughout a station's overall programming strategy with programs that are designed to accomplish this goal. The language of the act was sufficiently vague to avoid imposing any quantitative standards or minimum programming requirements, so stations began to redefine the purposes of their existing children's programs such as *The Jetsons, G.I. Joe,* and *Leave It to Beaver* as serving either the educational or the informational needs of children.

The FCC stepped into the fray in 1993 by declaring that such programming was not acceptable educational material, whereas broadcasters complained that their audiences would flock to the "the unregulated drivel on cable television" (Bogart 1995, 318).

---

11. The episode "I'll See You in Court" was slated for season 3 but never aired on Fox. It was later shown on the FX cable network. The episode has Al and Peggy Bundy visiting an adult motel where the proprietor secretly tapes his guests; in court, the judge rules that the sex was so brief that it could not be determined if the couple was even filmed having sex. Another episode, originally known as "A Period Piece," was heavily censored before airing as "The Camping Show." This episode features the Bundys camping with the next-door neighbors while all of the female characters experience their menstrual cycles.

The networks resisted for three years until President Bill Clinton brought broadcasters together on July 29, 1996. Clinton broke the impasse by getting the networks to agree to a schedule of three hours of programming per week to meet the educational needs of children sixteen and younger. The FCC met in August of that year, formally establishing the three-hour program requirement, which went into effect on September 1, 1997.

The Telecommunications Act of 1996

The Telecommunications Act of 1996 is the most recent attempt to both regulate and deregulate the television landscape as we know it. The act itself was written largely by employees of the various media companies, which Congress believed had conflicting goals because they competed with each other, yet that competition is at the core of a "free market." Media lobbyists assured congressional leaders that the act would increase competition, lower consumer prices, and make American media more globally competitive.

New content-based regulation came in the form of Section 551 of the act, which required that a "V-chip" be placed in all TV sets produced after 1999. Coupled with a voluntary age-based ratings system established for programming content that is broadcast ahead of a television program's signal, the V-chip allows broadcasters "to maintain self-regulation as the primary means of circumscribing media representations, thus minimizing direct state intervention; to empower parents as moral gatekeepers of the nation and thus uphold the right to privacy within the home; and to protect children and society from the presumed ill effects of violent and sexual programming" (Murray 1997, 315). Therefore, the V-chip, if used properly, effectively blocks any undesired television programming from being seen at all. Developed by broadcasters and cable operators as the easiest way to both let themselves off the hook and appease politicians and grassroots organizations, the television ratings system was introduced to the

American public. However, with most networks already employing fewer and fewer censors, the ratings system allows television program–content producers to put more and more objectionable material on television, arguing that the V-chip, not a Standards and Practices Department, is the new gatekeeper.

Despite the new television ratings system, there are still several notable problems. First, the age-based ratings provide almost no context and are ambiguous. Second, in a nation where many video cassette recorders still blink "12:00," setting up a television to utilize the V-chip technology is cumbersome and blocks adults from watching without entering a personal identification number. Third, the industry has done little in the way of educating the public about either the ratings or the fact that the public can use the V-chip to block programming, though the Janet Jackson Super Bowl incident did bring about some public service announcements. Fourth, for those viewers who simply do not (or cannot) program their televisions to use the V-chip, any unattended child can watch programming that is not intended for children.

Mergers Mergers Mergers

Although much of the public debate about the Telecommunications Act of 1996 centered on the V-chip, the bigger threat to free speech came in the sections of the law that the media underreported and on which the public had little input: the elimination of the limits on media ownership. Additionally, it seems that Congress intended the act to encourage cable operators to offer telephone service and broadcasters to offer cable service, permit local phone companies to offer long-distance service, as well as allow long-distance phone companies to offer local service, but where and how much competition Congress wanted may be questionable. Adding to the problem was that the Telecommunications Act of 1996 deregulated the public oversight of broadcasters by extending broadcast licenses from five to eight years for TV and from five to seven years for radio, with the first renewal for either virtually unchallengeable. Subsequent renewals have been made easier through barring challengers any hearing until the renewal question has been decided and makes it more difficult to challenge a renewal through the reduction of importance placed on public service programming.

Instead of fostering more competition in the television industry, the Telecommunications Act of 1996 actually reduced competition and diversity, because it required the FCC to relax its rules regarding media ownership. Despite the fact that there were only three networks before the introduction of Fox in 1987, the FCC had continued to relax its rules governing broadcast ownership, including repealing the "financial syndication" (or fin-syn) rules that had prevented networks from owning shows or participating in syndication profits.

By 2000, independent television stations had all but disappeared in a series of corporate buyouts and mergers, further reducing diversity of ownership. For example, Rupert Murdoch's News Corporation, owner of all things Fox, had lobbied hard for such deregulation and spent millions to ensure relaxation of the FCC's rules. In anticipation of the passage of the Telecommunications Act of 1996, Disney bought ABC, General Electric bought NBC, while Westinghouse divested itself of its industrial holdings and purchased CBS outright in 1995. The newly formed CBS Corporation then expanded by purchasing Infinity Broadcasting and the Nashville Network and Country Music Television cable channels, until CBS itself was purchased by Viacom while retaining the Eye Network's nomenclature.[12] The merger resulted in a company that controls the CBS Television Network, Nickelodeon, Showtime, MTV, Paramount Pictures, Simon and Schuster, and

---

12. On December 31, 2005, Viacom and the CBS Corporation split into two separate publicly traded companies controlled by National Amusements, which is in turn controlled by Sumner Redstone and his family.

Blockbuster Video, as well as the now defunct UPN Television Network,[13] producing the second largest U.S. media company.

The act also allowed for the merger of Time Warner, Turner Broadcasting, and America Online (AOL). The new company was briefly known as AOL Time Warner (and now just Time Warner, owing to AOL's recent downturn) and is a model of vertical integration, with CNN promoting *People, Time,* and *Sports Illustrated;* AOL promoting all things Time Warner, a cable operating system that has unfettered access to the Time Warner and MGM film libraries; Warner Television and Film divisions cross-promoting the parent company's assets; while their theme parks promote Warner Brothers cartoon characters.

Collectively, the combined influence of these four conglomerates (News Corporation, Disney, and CBS, coupled with five other companies) represents all of the major Hollywood film studios, all but one of five record labels that publish 90 percent of U.S. music, most of America's book publishers, the owners of nearly every commercially successful cable channel, the owners of the majority of television stations in the top fifteen markets, and the owners of all five U.S. television networks. Most recently, NBC went on a buying spree, purchasing the Bravo television network and, more important, Vivendi Universal, a megamerger designed to compete with the likes of Disney and CBS. Invariably, this sort of ownership of media outlets has led, inevitably, to corporate censorship, in which the needs of shareholders outweigh the rights of the public.

The Year 2004: Historic Events Step In

Although every television program has the possibility of offending portions of its audience, and portions of that audience may

---

13. The UPN and the WB networks merged in 2006 to form the CW, presumably to share in a larger piece of an ever dwindling pie of network viewership.

or may not do more than switch channels, certain broadcasts can spawn massive reactions. In 2004, one such broadcast event focused the nation's attention on the television networks with regards to censorship and indecency and sparked a new round of legislative attempts to curb content on both television and radio. Driving this renewed interest was, primarily, Janet Jackson's now infamous "wardrobe malfunction" during the live broadcast of the 2004 Super Bowl halftime show, in which her right breast was shown live on television for a mere eighteen frames, or less than three-quarters of a second. Contrast this event to a scene in a March 2003 episode of ABC's *NYPD Blue,* in which "a total of 11.6 million viewers saw *Blue*'s boldest nude scene yet—nearly 20 seconds' worth of lingering shots of [Charlotte] Ross's curvy body as she twirled and struggled to cover (ineffectually) her naughty bits. Yet, according to ABC, only a handful of viewers called the network to complain" (Daly 2003, 28). Also adding fuel to this fire was the use of the word *fucking* by U2's lead singer, Bono, during the live broadcast of the 2003 Golden Globes awards ceremony.[14] Like the Super Bowl incident, Bono's utterance was aired live—yet NBC reported that not one viewer called to complain about it.

Originally, the FCC deemed Bono's use of the word acceptable because he had used it as an adjective in a nonsexual way, but political pressure forced the agency to reverse itself in the post–Janet Jackson era. The combination of the two incidents now means that "live" events such as the Oscars and the Emmys are tape-delayed in order to catch—and prevent—any obscenities from being broadcast.

The corporate reaction to the public outcry over Janet Jackson's Super Bowl appearance was widespread. Radio "shock jocks" across the country were told to curb their speech or were

---

14. Upon taking the stage to accept the Golden Globe for Best Song, Bono said, "This is really, really fucking brilliant."

otherwise shown the curb, as the FCC and Congress raised indecency fines tenfold. Infamous shock-jock Howard Stern escaped increasing scrutiny by moving to satellite radio for an obscene amount of cash.[15] Meanwhile, the cable industry launched an educational campaign that includes television spots aimed at explaining to parents how they can block unwanted programming, as well as printed materials in subscribers' bills. And then the FCC proposed a $3.6 million fine for the CBS program *Without a Trace* for a 2006 episode that featured an orgy scene.[16] Collectively, all of this new congressional attention has worried broadcasters, which can have a chilling effect on their programming decisions with regards to controversial content in the future, especially since some members in Congress are calling for an expansion of the FCC to incorporate cable and satellite transmissions.

A Brief Outline of the Book

In my examination of American television network censorship of programming content from 1967 to 2002, there are four programs on which this book will focus: *The Smothers Brothers Comedy Hour (TSBCH), The Richard Pryor Show (TRPS), TV Nation (TVN),* and *Politically Incorrect with Bill Maher (PI).* I have chosen these four shows because they were all controversial in their day, and collectively they represent the four largest broadcast networks in operation in the United States.

Chapter 2 examines *The Smothers Brothers Comedy Hour,* focusing on the controversies surrounding the CBS series that ran from

15. The five-year deal was reportedly worth up to five hundred million dollars for Stern.

16. As of April 2007, CBS was challenging the fine, based on the fact that none of the 4,211 who e-mailed petitions provided by the Parents Television Council (PTC) had viewed the program in question. The PTC is not a grassroots organization but a subsidiary of the Media Research Group, a conservative think tank.

1967 to 1969. As the program became more and more politicized, aligning itself with the countercultural movement, CBS executives felt pressure to quiet the Smothers Brothers, resulting in a very public fight over censorship. Despite being canceled by CBS over the program's content, *The Smothers Brothers Comedy Hour* went on to win the 1969 Emmy for Outstanding Writing Achievement in Comedy, Variety, or Music.

Chapter 3 looks at the ill-fated *Richard Pryor Show,* which ran for just four episodes on NBC in the fall of 1977. NBC heavily lobbied Richard Pryor after the network aired a very successful special in the spring of 1977 and made a full-court press for him to sign up for a regular program, despite knowing that his fame came from his extremely profane comedy routine (and the albums it spawned).

Chapter 4 examines Michael Moore's *TV Nation,* a summer replacement series that ran on NBC in 1994 and then on Fox in the summer of 1995. Both networks fought censorship battles with the program's creator, documentary filmmaker Michael Moore, who had basically told both networks that he would turn his cameras on the show's sponsors. Despite its relatively short run on NBC, *TV Nation* won an Emmy for Outstanding Informational Series in 1994.

Chapter 5 looks at *Politically Incorrect with Bill Maher,* tracing the program's rise from cable obscurity to network darling and back again—owing in no small part to Bill Maher's controversial remarks that led to a sponsor-led boycott of the program.

Chapter 6 will examine the commonality that exists among these programs, followed by a discussion of the future of network programming and censorship and the impact that media conglomeration will have on what is ultimately shown to broadcast television audiences in the United States.

2 Tuned In, Turned On, Then Kicked Off

The Smothers Brothers Comedy Hour

A Youthful Folk-Song Act

On Sunday, February 5, 1967, at 9:00 P.M. eastern time, *The Smothers Brothers Comedy Hour* aired for the first time to phenomenal ratings. The show's premise was simple enough: take the very successful folksinging and comedy act that was the Smothers Brothers, and turn it into a variety show in an attempt to counter-program the perennial Nielsen ratings champ *Bonanza*, the number-one program for three straight seasons (McNeil 1991; Brooks and Marsh 1999).[1] The program eventually accomplished that task, knocking *Bonanza* from first to sixth place by the end of its second season. Despite such success, *TSBCH* rode a whirlwind of controversy that eventually led to its own demise—and sparked "the biggest debate on network censorship in the medium's history" (Brooks 1987, 937). The controversy from this breakthrough program paved the way for politically and socially conscious programs such as *All in the Family, M*A*S*H,* and *Saturday Night Live*—programs that entered the mainstream through both initial

1. *Bonanza* was the Nielsen highest-rated program for the 1964–1965, 1965–1966, and 1966–1967 seasons (see Brooks and Marsh 1999).

commercial success and acceptance as well as the highly lucrative syndication market.

Given the sudden and publicly devastating demise of *TSBCH* in April 1969, contrasted with the longer-running successor for the countercultural audience that was NBC's *Laugh-In*, the modern viewer is left to wonder what was so controversial that merited the Smothers Brothers' firing, a question that still needs to be answered. By placing the program in historical perspective, however, one begins to see a much different picture. In the mid- to late 1960s, bland programs such as *The Andy Griffith Show, Gilligan's Island, The Beverly Hillbillies, Green Acres,* and *Gomer Pyle, U.S.M.C.* were CBS's standard family fare. These programs offered very little in the way of controversy; in fact, Gomer Pyle's depiction of Marine Corps life was uncharacteristically unrealistic for the late 1960s—his training seems centered on cleaning barracks, not preparing for a tour in Vietnam, which was purposely never mentioned on the program.[2] The network's violent programming, found in shows such as *Mission: Impossible, Gunsmoke,* and *Mannix,* was beginning to fall under the specter of pending federal legislation, led by Senator John Pastore of Rhode Island, to expand the government's role in censoring network television.

The reactions at all three networks were typified by the response of CBS president Frank Stanton, who believed that it was a network's place to censor its programming, not the government's.[3]

2. Vietnam would eventually get passing references on CBS's crime drama *Hawaii Five-O,* which began airing in 1968, particularly because of the military's "rest and relaxation" jaunts that it provided to military personnel in Hawaii. These shows were in the post–Tet Offensive era, when growing public scrutiny of the war became more commonplace, and the soldiers depicted were usually portrayed in a negative light.

3. Frank Stanton was appointed president of CBS by William Paley, serving in that role from 1946 until his forced retirement in 1973. According to his executrix (in a telephone conversation in November 2006), Stanton destroyed all

Stanton actively fought all attempts at what he saw as governmental intrusion into private enterprise. Into this atmosphere of tight corporate control (naively) entered the Smothers Brothers, who, in their trademark red blazers, buzz-cut hair, and playful takes on folk music, offered what seemed to be a safe alternative to the growing counterculture of sex, drugs, and rock and roll. They were safe, and their college-circuit folksinging act had an element that many of today's mass-media producers and writers find critical—reality—because, as Tom put it, "performers should reflect the times they live in" (Whitney 1968, 19). Yet by the end of the decade, after two and a half years of struggling against the network brass, the Smothers Brothers were removed from the air because—despite their success as humorists and clowns (both critically and commercially)—they were deemed to be unfit to provide social commentary by the network.

Yet the late 1960s saw an increase in public activism—from the Vietnam War to segregation—that sparked Free Speech Movements and a (what is now seen as healthy) debate over the breadth and depth of the First Amendment. Some scholars thought that the public also had a growing concern not only of governmental censorship but also of corporate censorship—the very type of constraint that the Hutchins Commission had warned against back in 1947. With respect to *TSBCH*, such constraints came in the form of censorship not only of verboten words but of ideas that Tom and Dick Smothers tried to introduce on their program as well. As the show increasingly embraced the countercultural movement, it pushed CBS's Program Practices Department each week by defiantly featuring McCarthy-era blacklisted performers and folksingers, little-known psychedelic acid-rock bands, and

---

of his personal notes from CBS several years earlier at his discretion and before he became too ill to attend to them. Stanton passed away on December 24, 2006, at the age of ninety-eight.

critical sketch comedy that took aim at the current events that were normally found on the network's newscasts: gun control, Vietnam, and the presidency.

Enter Two Clean-Cut Kids: Season 1, 1967

The first season of the program started off fairly innocently. The humor was, for the most part, kept at the sophomoric level that was the Smothers Brothers coffeehouse and college-circuit stage act—an act that CBS found acceptable and believed was capable of winning the eighteen- to thirty-four-year-old age group. Reflecting on the early days of the program, Tom Smothers said during a rebroadcast of the February 26, 1967, episode that "there was no censorship in the first four weeks of the show."[4] At first, the only controversial elements the program really had (and what originally attracted the youth market) were its musical guests: Jefferson Airplane, Buffalo Springfield, the Electric Prunes, the Blue Magoos, the Turtles, Sonny and Cher, and Simon and Garfunkel—all of whom appeared in the first season. These acts were sharply contrasted by the traditional, established guest stars that CBS supplied: George Burns, Jack Benny, Jimmy Durante, Bob Crane, Martin Landau and Barbara Bain, Tony Randall, Bette Davis, and Janet Leigh.

A source of continued controversy began with one of cast member Pat Paulsen's earliest editorials. In his editorial on the March 19, 1967, episode, Paulsen addressed the issue of gun control: "Many people today are suggesting that restrictions be placed on the purchase and ownership of firearms. No one questions that these people are like all of us, good, solid Americans. They are either grossly misinformed and hence misguided—or

---

4. *TSBCH* had not been seen in syndication since it had aired. In 1992, the E! Television Cable Network rebroadcast the program, adding interviews and commentary from cast members and guest stars.

else they are trouble-making Communists. But we respect them. And we will fight to the death against their right to express opinions."[5] "It's about our inalienable right to kill. . . . Very straight double-talk," Tom explained at the time, and the episode received 7,500 requests for reprints (Stone 1969, 21). The Smothers Brothers continued with the debate on gun control and what could (and could not) be seen on television on the May 14, 1967, episode with the "Billy the Kid Birthday" sketch. Billy, played by Tom, takes hold of Janet Leigh, exclaiming that he would rather make love than kill, but he is interrupted by Pat Paulsen (playing Doc Holiday), who says, "That's disgusting." The actor playing Bat Masterson explains, "You can kill on television, but you can't make love." Tom's simple reaction: "That's weird."

The first major run-in with network censorship came, ironically enough, with a skit about movie censors, authored by Elaine May, that was to air on the April 9, 1967, episode. The sketch features May and Tom revising the following line, "My heart beats wildly in my chest when you are near," to "My pulse beats wildly in my wrist when you are near." Mason Williams, head writer and performer, recalls the original line was *breast*, but it was changed to *chest* in an attempt to appease the censors.[6] Another scene, concerning a college biology class learning about the mating habits of earthworms, concerns the fictional censors of the skit as well. Judy Stone, writing for the *New York Times*, wrote that "in a case of life imitating art, there was much fussing and frowning at CBS over airing unmentionables as 'breast' and 'heterosexual' and the life cycle of the worm," whereas Tom Smothers angrily quipped, "The censors censored the censorship bit" (21). Mason Williams, one of the program's writers, recalled the sentiments

5. I transcribed all show quotations presented in this book from tapes of the broadcasts.

6. Mason Williams, personal communication, February 22, 2007.

at the network regarding the April 9, 1967, episode: "What they really didn't want the public to be made aware of was the fact that censorship was involved and one of the things we did was to personify the censor."[7]

According to Tommy Smothers, network executives told the brothers that the skit was in "bad taste," which "left me with a great deal of disrespect for them as far as their taste is concerned and you can quote me on that" (21). Although the country did not get to see the sketch, Tom Smothers made certain that his loss of creative control did not go unnoticed. He rocked the boat by calling the press and publishing a transcript of the censorship sketch in the *New York Times*.

"Waist Deep in the Big Muddy": Season 2, 1967–1968

For the first episode of the 1967–1968 season, the Smothers Brothers "received" permission to have Pete Seeger as one of their guests. Ernest Chambers, one of the program's producers, told the *New York Times* at the time, "We decided to put him on the season's first program because it is the most significant thing we'll do all year"—a premature statement that did not take into account Seeger's choice of material (Dallos 1967, 72).[8] For his first appearance on commercial television since 1950, Seeger chose to perform "Waist Deep in the Big Muddy," which was seen as an antiwar protest song; however, it was CBS's policy at the time not to permit what it believed to be controversial material in its prime-time entertainment programming. Seeger had released the song on his album of the same name on CBS Records, the irony of which was not lost on those individuals involved at the time: that it was legitimate to exploit Seeger in one medium (records) while

7. Rebroadcast interview for E! in 1992.

8. For a more thorough account of Pete Seeger's experiences with CBS, see Spector 1983.

banning him from another (television). Although the majority of the song concerns the experiences of an infantry platoon during World War II, what concerned the network censors was the sixth stanza, which was believed to be directed at Lyndon Johnson's Vietnam policies:

> But every time I read the papers
> That old feeling comes on
> We're waist deep in the Big Muddy
> And the big fool says to push on.[9]

Despite changing sentiments in the country toward the war, the segment was cut—creating a stir about the song itself.

Although Pete Seeger did not appear on the American broadcast of the September 24, 1967, episode, some antiwar sentiment did make it onto that broadcast, and the entire segment ran uncut on the privately owned Canadian Television Network. According to Tom Smothers, *TSBCH* ran uncut and unedited in Canada for the duration of the program.[10] In his closing remarks on the September 24, 1967, episode, Tom says, "Hello to all of the Americans living up in Canada" in the hopes that they will return "if not this November, perhaps next year," a reference to both draft dodgers who had escaped the draft by moving to Canada and the upcoming presidential election of 1968.

By Pete Seeger's second appearance, the network had had a change of heart, the subculture had inched forward, and the country finally got to see and hear "Waist Deep in the Big Muddy" on February 25, 1968, in its entirety—except for viewers of Detroit's WJBK-TV, which cut "Waist Deep" from its broadcast of the show. In 1992, Pete Seeger explained the origin of the song:

9. Seeger 1967. Lyrics copyright © 1967 (renewed) by Melody Trails, Inc., New York, N.Y. Used by permission.

10. Rebroadcast interview for E! in 1992.

I voted for Lyndon Johnson. . . . A few months after, he escalated the war. Such a shrewd man—he could have easily stood up and said, "Fellow Americans, the electorate has spoken. Let's pull our troops home and make this a better country and let the Vietnamese settle their own quarrels themselves." Instead, he dug his own grave, and the grave of hundreds and thousands of others—Americans, Vietnamese, and others. And when I saw a picture in the newspaper of some troops slogging through some river in the Mekong Delta, one line came to me all at once: "Waist deep in the Big Muddy, and the big fool says to push on."[11]

The Smothers Brothers continued to reach out to and identify with the antiestablishment counterculture with the introduction of Leigh French's hippie character, "Goldie." The character began as a drugged-out "audience member," but as "flower power" began to take the country by storm, Goldie earned her own segment on the program. On the September 24, 1967, episode, Tom pulls Goldie out of the audience. When Tom thanks her for coming down onstage, Goldie replies, "I didn't come down. I never come down," and presents Tom with a special necklace:

GOLDIE: I made it myself. I grew it myself.
TOM: Are they beads?
GOLDIE: No, they're seeds.

George Burns was a guest on this episode as well, singing the Beatles' "Day Tripper" in vaudevillian style. When he finished, he turned to the camera and asked the audience, "What is a day tripper?" In asking this question, Burns spoke to his generation

11. Ibid.

as well as "square" America in trying to figure out the growing drug-culture lexicon.[12]

Part of the brothers' shtick was for Tom to say or do something in his "simpleton" form, and Dick would often interrupt their routine in order to call Tom on the carpet for his indiscretion. In the opening song for the February 18, 1968, episode, Tom sings "Marijuana que fumar" during their rendition of "La Cucaracha." Here, the obvious drug reference to roaches (la cucaracha) and marijuana "roaches" is seen. Later on the same episode was a "Share a Little Tea with Goldie" sketch, in which she offers viewers a "beautiful lesson" so that we can "really look at each other and dig each other." On this episode Goldie is drinking coffee, but a sudden loss of audio—even on the 1992 rerun of uncut episodes—is an example of how close she came to being completely censored. At the end of the skit, Goldie asks viewers to send her any "groovy hints" by rolling them up and sending them in, and she promises, "We'll share it"—an obvious reference to a marijuana joint.

This episode also features Herman's Hermits, who participate in the "Little Red Robin Hood" sketch, with Pat Paulsen as the sheriff of Nottingham. When Robin Hood (played by Tom) questions the sheriff of Nottingham as to where he got the gun he pulled, Paulsen responds, "Through the mail"—a reference to his own editorial, and quite possibly to the claim that Lee Harvey Oswald purchased his Manlicher through the mail.

12. In British lexicon, a "day-tripper" was initially a lower-middle-class term for one who traveled for a one-day excursion, usually to Land's End by train. In the growing counterculture of the late 1960s, "tripping" was used by the drug culture, typically referring to "tripping on acid" (LSD). As the Beatles themselves delved more and more into drugs, the song was seen as having a dual meaning, despite their insistence that it was coincidental. Another example was "Lucy in the Sky with Diamonds," the main words of the title also coincidentally spelling out "LSD."

According to what the Smothers Brothers called a "big-daddy memo," a sketch that was to appear on the May 28, 1968, episode, was cut. According to CBS executives, "The Apple sketch will only be acceptable after the deletion of 'That's a no-no' delivered by the disembodied voice. It can only be interpreted as the Voice of God and as such must be considered irreverent" (Whitney 1968, 15). To paraphrase David Steinberg (who would later be chastised for his sermonettes of the 1968–1969 season), it wouldn't be funny if it weren't irreverent.

Also featured on the May 28, 1968, episode was a satirical skit about young George Washington. At one point in the skit, Washington asks, "What's a president?" to which Tom's character explains, "Well, it's like a king, except you wear a regular suit and a big cowboy hat if you want to," an obvious reference to Johnson.

Beeping Censors Lurkin' in the Wings: Season 3, 1968–1969

Tom and Dick drew a line in the sand with their opening song of the first episode of the third and final season of *TSBCH* on CBS:

> The war in Vietnam keeps on a-raging,
> Blacks and whites still haven't worked it out
> Pollution, guns, and poverty surround us
> No wonder everybody's droppin' out.
> Chorus:
> But we're still here, oh yeah
> We're still here.
> We face the same ol' problems
> That weekly gripe is stretchin' out before us
> Beeping censors lurkin' in the wings
> CBS would like to give us notice
> And some of you don't like the things we say.

(Chorus)
You may not think we're funny, but we're still here
Oh, both of us have grown a manly moustache
The blazers we always wore are gone
Our clean-cut all-American look is changin'
But underneath we're still old Dick and Tom
(Chorus)
You may not recognize us, but we're still here.[13]

As a time capsule of not only the problems of the show but also the year 1968, this song captures the antiestablishment's thoughts concerning American life. The reference to "droppin' out" as a reaction to the Vietnam War, pollution, and poverty is clearly a reference to Timothy Leary's (in)famous statement of "tune in, turn on, and drop out." The new image the brothers present—in which their blazers are gone and they have grown facial hair—was radical for television, and especially for those individuals close to thirty at the time (Tom was thirty-one, Dick twenty-nine).

Although the 1967–1968 season was controversial, what was to become the final season of the program would push CBS censors and management past the breaking point. The third-season episodes exhibited a marked difference from the first two seasons, owing largely to the fact that Tom and Dick had assumed the role of executive producers. Jimmy Durante, Kate Smith, and George Burns made way for the Committee, George Carlin, Jackie Mason, and Mort Sahl.[14] Just as the previous season began with censorship of a controversial singer, so too did the 1968–1969 season.

13. *TSBCH,* September 29, 1968.

14. The Committee was a West Coast comedy troupe that originated in San Francisco (and had a branch in Los Angeles between 1967 and 1970), whose members at the time included Peter Bonerz, Howard Hesseman, Rob Reiner, and Carl Gottleib; the latter two worked as writers during the show's last season.

The first episode was to have featured Harry Belafonte singing "Don't Stop the Carnival," a song written about and set to film footage from the 1968 Democratic National Convention. The entire segment was cut—forcing the Smothers Brothers to extend their question-and-answer period with the audience. Harry Belafonte later stated, "I would rather have the Smothers Brothers on the air for the length of time we did saying something than to have them on forever saying nothing." Looking at the episode today, it is obvious that Tom is rattled as he tries to explain why the question-and-answer period will run long, and even suggests to viewers that they tune in to *Bonanza.* Tom later recalled that what compounded the situation was CBS's decision to cut the extended rap session altogether and sell the airtime to Richard Nixon's campaign for a paid political announcement, raising the stakes in Tom's eyes.[15]

Aside from the political ramifications of this episode, the Smother Brothers also pushed the limits of what was considered "foul language." In a spoof of *Bonanza,* Cass Elliot plays Hass (a play on her name and Dan Blocker's Hoss), and the skit features a series of bleeped lines, such as "You're a wise, Hass [bleep]" and "Don't grab that, Hass [bleep]." The plot of the skit reflected a growing criticism of the "Smut Brothers," played by Tom and Dick, who have taken the "Nielsen family" hostage, and Tom questions the unintentionally implied homosexuality of *Bonanza:* "Two guys ain't bad, but three is kind of [bleep]."

For the October 27, 1968, episode, the brothers had comedian David Steinberg perform his sermonette on Moses, which garnered immediate negative reaction from both the public and CBS. In the monologue, Steinberg jokes that Moses burned his feet at the burning bush and claims that "there are many Old Testament scholars who to this day believe it was the first mention of Christ

15. Rebroadcast interview for E! in 1992.

in the Bible," then closes the sermonette with a more recent anec-
dote: "Perhaps I can best illustrate my point with something I saw
this evening. As I was on my way to the theater, I saw an old man
I would take to be eighty to eighty-five years old. And this old
man was being badly beaten by four little children. And I couldn't
help but notice that one child was a Negro, one was Jewish, one
was Spanish, and yet another, Italian. Now . . . if these little children can learn to play together, then why can't the world? Thank
you." Although Steinberg had performed the piece previously on
NBC's *Tonight Show,* the entire monologue was deemed inappropriate for CBS's Sunday-evening audience, prompting CBS to ban
any further sermonettes by Steinberg on the program.

Later in the season, in a show of its power, CBS forced Tom to
make a public apology for the first David Steinberg sermonette on
the November 17, 1968, episode. Much to the chagrin of the CBS
brass, Tom also remarked that he did not regret airing the piece
in the first place. Later, as a show of solidarity with the brothers,
George Harrison appeared on the episode, telling the brothers to
"Keep trying to say it." As the season progressed, Tom maintained
that CBS and its censors were continuing to harass the Smothers
Brothers and the production of their program.

The following week, the show prominently featured a popular
antiwar poster, "War is not healthy for children and other living
things," during the production. Also during this episode, Tony
Randall was featured in a Western Union skit. Like a postal car-
rier, Randall fights snow and strong wind to deliver a telegram.
Just as he crosses the Canadian border, Randall delivers this poi-
gnant (and now dated) line: "Gee, Canada—this is a great place
to get out of the draft."[16]

If there is one episode in particular that would shock the American public during the third season, the December 8, 1968, episode

16. *TSBCH,* November 24, 1968.

would be the most likely candidate, as it introduced the public to the cast and music of the West Coast production of *Hair*. Today, it is almost impossible to imagine the stir created by twenty long-haired "freaks" singing "The Age of Aquarius" before a national audience; however, Tom would later recall that the show came close to losing its production crew when the cameramen refused to tape a segment because an actor had allowed the American flag to touch the ground.[17]

As the tumultuous year 1968 came to a close, *TSBCH* continued to mirror the year's turmoil and remained a representative of the counterculture. At the beginning of the December 15, 1968, episode, Tom is seen putting on a gas mask, riot helmet, and riot gloves. Dick asks him what he is doing. Tom replies, "I'm getting ready to go to college."

Comedian Jackie Mason later recalled that the Smothers Brothers hired him even though he had been blacklisted by Ed Sullivan (who also appeared on CBS).[18] Mason's humor on the January 19, 1969, episode called into question the government's official statements about Vietnam as exaggerations: "Every day, they say we knocked out five hundred bridges in North Vietnam. I studied North Vietnam—there are only eight bridges in North Vietnam." By this time, Lyndon Johnson was closing out his presidency, and

17. Rebroadcast interview for E! in 1992. Tom was partly responsible for bringing *Hair* to the West Coast in 1968 with his production partners. *Hair* had opened only recently at the newly renovated (and renamed) Aquarius Theater before the production members appeared on *TSBCH*. For the uninitiated, despite the many high school productions that alter certain scenes, *Hair* was (and is) a countercultural musical that openly featured full-frontal nudity, draft-card burning, and drug use. The play originally opened off-Broadway in 1967. The feature-length film, directed by Milos Forman, was not made until 1979.

18. Ibid. What makes Mason's hiring so much more intriguing is that *The Ed Sullivan Show* was the lead-in show for *TSBCH*. Mason had been barred by Sullivan in 1962 for supposedly giving Sullivan the finger on live TV.

although Richard Nixon and his secret plan for the Vietnam War had not reached office, *TSBCH* continued steadfastly in its view of the draft and the war in general. In the "Minority Report" presented on the same episode, a "man-on-the-street" character named Mr. Harris (played by Mel Stewart) is asked whether the draft laws are fair to blacks: "I believe that the draft laws show no racial discrimination whatsoever. In fact, I believe that the black man has an even better opportunity to be drafted than the white man. And the equality does not stop there. Why, back here at home, we are sometimes asked to ride in the back of the bus, but when we're called into the armed services, we're moved immediately to the front. Now that's more than equal opportunity."[19] This stance reflected the reality of the fighting in Vietnam: more than half of all frontline ground troops were African American, a lopsided percentage, since African Americans made up between only 10.5 percent and 11.1 percent of the U.S. population between 1960 and 1970 (Coffey 1990; U.S. Bureau of the Census 1999).

Also featured on the January 19, 1969, episode was a segment titled "How Has the Draft Affected You?" another parody of the "man-on-the-street" features prevalent in the news at the time. In the sketch, a group of typical American mothers are asked this question, and the group's spokeswoman replies (rather straitlacedly), "We mothers gather in each other's houses to read our sons' mail, and it comes from all over: Winnipeg, Toronto, Montreal." Such a response in 1969 was seen as unpatriotic and un-American by many Americans and was a very difficult and painful issue well into the 1970s, as it was not until President Carter's blanket pardon of draft dodgers that the issue was, at least politically, laid to rest.

19. Mel Stewart is perhaps best known to television audiences as Henry Jefferson, George Jefferson's brother who sparred often with Archie Bunker on *All in the Family* (1971–1973).

Just after Richard Nixon took office, the Smothers Brothers wasted no time in aiming their satiric sights on the new president, as the February 16, 1969, episode shows. In a long, satiric piece titled "A Fable for Our Time," a political fairy tale features a declining "King Johnson," who must choose a successor between his three sons, Humphrey, Wallace, and Nixon. At one point, the king says he "never wanted to send boys on crusades," much in line with Johnson's real regrets for sending troops into Vietnam. Prince Nixon, of course, tells his "father" that he has a secret plan for recalling the crusades, and thus wins the crown from the other candidates.

Renewed for 1969–1970, Then Fired

Despite a long and bitter history of disagreements with management and censorship issues, *The Smothers Brothers Comedy Hour* was renewed for the 1969–1970 season on March 14, 1969; however, what transpired during the following three weeks led to a change of heart at the network. During this time, Tom was in Washington, D.C., attending the annual NAB convention, where he also courted members of the FCC and congressional officials. While in Washington, Tom was (ironically) encouraged by a speech given by then CBS president Frank Stanton. In the speech, Stanton drew a line in the sand, asserting that CBS would challenge Senator John Pastore's proposal for pre-screening of questionable programs by a national review board. At the time, Stanton said that "an outside agency wielding the blue pencil would throttle the creative impulses which are essential to the continuing improvement of TV. . . . The creators of our programs need encouragement and stimulation, not the reverse" (R. Lewis 1969, 184).

In a congratulatory response to what seemed to be a complete reversal of CBS policy toward his program, Tom sent Stanton a telegram that the brothers had agreed to continue for a fourth season at CBS, "so they could retain a platform to continue their push for new standards of broadcast content" (184). Upon his return to California, Tom told *Daily Variety* that "he was encouraged by everything he had heard in Washington, and hoped to help CBS raise their standards of program acceptability to include more relevant material and more youth-oriented programming" (Kloman 1969, 149). In response, CBS president Robert Wood sent a three-foot-long Telex wire to the brothers on March 27. Wood explained that Tom had misunderstood Stanton's speech, in that Stanton was defending CBS's intention to police itself: "YOU ARE NOT FREE TO USE "THE SMOTHERS BROTHERS COMEDY HOUR" AS A DEVICE TO PUSH FOR NEW STANDARDS. IF YOU CANNOT COMPLY WITH OUR STANDARDS THE [SHOW] CANNOT APPEAR ON CBS. . . . WE CANNOT MAKE AN EXCEPTION OF THE "SMOTHERS BROTHERS" SHOW NOR CAN WE LOWER OUR PROGRAM STANDARDS. THE NETWORK CANNOT IGNORE ITS RESPONSIBILITIES TO THE PUBLIC TO MAINTAIN CERTAIN STANDARDS" (R. Lewis 1969, 191).

The Episode That Killed the Brothers

At the time the Smothers Brothers were fired, all three networks had a policy of allowing their affiliates to prescreen programs upon request. However, CBS was the only network to insist on such a screening for each episode of *TSBCH* after the first Steinberg sermonette that aired on the October 27, 1968, episode, after which the network barred Steinberg from delivering any further sermonettes on the program. The Smothers reluctantly accepted this practice and began shipping tapes on the Thursday before they were to be aired so they could be prescreened by CBS affiliates.

Taping of what was meant to be the April 13, 1969, episode was completed just after the lengthy Wood tome was received by the Smothers, and the show featured another sermonette by David Steinberg in which Steinberg exclaims that Jonah was thrown overboard because "the Gentiles, as they are wont from time to time, threw the Jew overboard."[20]

CBS got wind of the scheduled appearance of the verboten performer and asked for and received an advance copy of the second Steinberg sermonette. Normally, with at least two weeks to edit and prepare a show, this kind of demand from the network Program Practices Department would not have caused much trouble. However, in a strange twist of fate and what would ultimately be the final blow to the show itself, CBS informed the brothers on Friday, March 28, 1969, that because Dan Rowan was scheduled to appear on an NBC special on April 13, the network wanted to avoid having the guest star appear against himself, and this courtesy required moving the program to April 6. By Wednesday, April 2, the Smotherses' attorney received word that the Steinberg sermonette would have to be cut to meet network standards, leaving a four-minute gap in the show. With such a late request for editing, the earliest Tom could comply with this request was Thursday, April 3. In delivering the tape by messenger to CBS in Los Angeles on Thursday and by air express to New York for screening on Friday, Tom believed he was in loose compliance at best and innocent breach at worst of his contractual obligation to CBS to submit tapes to both the Los Angeles and the New York Program Practices Departments for prescreening. However, Wood had, correctly or not, reminded the Smotherses in his March 27 telegram that tapes would be required by the Wednesday before a broadcast, although no such clause could be found in the brothers' contract with CBS. With such a conflicting sequence of events, the "breach of contract" that Wood claims seems to have been created solely by CBS and its Program Practices Department.

---

20. Because of a scheduling conflict, the episode was moved up to April 6, 1969, but never aired on CBS. Although the program was broadcast in Canada, it did not appear on American television until 1992, on the E! Television Network.

By Friday, April 4, the preview tapes were in the hands of CBS on both coasts. Meanwhile, Tom was on a trip to San Francisco, where he and his brother were planning to move the program for the 1969–1970 season, when he was notified by telegram that they had been fired. The story broke the next day, as the following headline ran on the front page of the April 5, 1969, edition of the *New York Times:* "C.B.S. to Drop Smothers Hour: Cites Failure to Get Previews." In his April 4 telegram to the Smotherses, Wood cited receiving the late review tape as a habitual problem, calling it a breach of contract and grounds for termination. Wood placed additional emphasis on the second David Steinberg sermonette—which had, in fact, been cut two days earlier from the preview tape in CBS's possession. Regardless, Wood claimed the sermonette would have been deemed inappropriate in any given week, but especially so since it would have aired after General Eisenhower's funeral on Easter Sunday. Even with the Steinberg sermonette cut from the tape, CBS decided not to air the episode, because the rest of the tape was seen as being in bad taste. The CBS version of the story also appeared on the front page of the April 5, 1969, edition of the *New York Times* as well as in a special editorial in *TV Guide,* which wrote in favor of CBS on April 15, 1969. It should be noted that *TV Guide* was owned by Walter Annenberg at the time, a staunch Goldwater conservative and later named as Nixon's ambassador to the Court of St. James.

The troubled episode was later shown in Canada and received rave reviews—even from critics of the program, such as Jack Gould of the *New York Times,* who pointed out that the censored episode was the only one produced by the three networks that bothered to observe the first anniversary of Martin Luther King Jr.'s assassination (Gould 1969). Despite several articles in national magazines that favored the Smothers Brothers' version of the events leading to their dismissal (Henthoff 1969; Leonard 1969), the story began to fade from the public's memory. More important, because the Smothers Brothers were off the air and without a weekly nationally televised soapbox, the myth that *The Smothers Brothers Comedy Hour* was canceled for not meeting contractual obligations—rather than the brothers being fired for rocking the boat—still persists.

What Was Controversial

In reviewing the entire run of *TSBCH*, the principal basis for CBS's objections came down primarily to who ultimately had creative control of the program. In their original contract, the Smothers Brothers were given full creative license, though their understanding of this latitude in light of the control that CBS's Program Practices Department had at the time seems a bit naive. No matter how much creative control was given, at the end of the day CBS had the ultimate right to air or not air what was provided to it. The Smothers Brothers, who started off as a college folk act, kept their fingers on the pulse of the youth in the United States because that was their primary audience. In the late 1960s, a highly vocal part of this audience was interested in civil rights, the draft, and the Vietnam War. Rather than avoiding these issues, the Smothers Brothers tried to address them every week on national television. The result was a hit series for CBS, as evidenced by the fact that the fourth season's advertising allotment was nearly sold out. The rest of CBS's objections, ranging from airing new psychedelic rock bands, blacklisted performers, gun-control issues, and drug humor to aiming the show at the antiestablishment youth movement, all stem from this central argument over creative control and where the network wanted to position itself with respect to these issues. The principal fight was not over words (although those boundaries were pushed as well) but over ideas that the network found objectionable. That the brothers objected to CBS's heavy-handed approach of the work of these censors, both on and off the program, eventually led to their termination from the network.

Network versus Governmental Censorship

"We weren't canceled. We were fired," recalled Tom in an interview for the rebroadcast of the April 6, 1969, episode that never aired on CBS. When all was finally said and done, the net result was that *TSBCH* was off the air, and the Smothers Brothers' career was put on hold—and some might even say ruined—by their breach-of-contract lawsuit with CBS. Meanwhile, government-mandated censorship, in the form of pending legislation by Senator Pastore, never came to pass. Eventually, network television began to put socially conscious television programming on the air—the most notable of which, ironically, was CBS's *All in the Family* in 1971.

Six days after the brothers were fired, then FCC chairman Nicholas Johnson was quoted in the *New York Times* with regards to the state of censorship in the United States: "The stifling weight of censorship is not to be found in the hearing rooms of the Federal Communications Commission, but in the conference rooms of this nation's largest television networks" ("TV-Industry View" 1969, 47). CBS, for its part, never aired the April 6, 1969, episode, airing instead a repeat of the November 10, 1968, episode that contained the following poem (titled "The Censor") by Mason Williams, which, ironically, brought the fight over censorship, and censors, to the American public:

> The Censor sits
> Somewhere between
> The scenes to be seen
> And the television sets
> With his scissor purpose poised
> Watching the human stuff
> That will sizzle through
> The magic wires
> And light up

Like welding shops
The ho-hum rooms of America
And with a kindergarten
Arts and crafts concept
Of moral responsibility
Snips out
The rough talk
The unpopular opinion
Or anything with teeth
And renders
A pattern of ideas
Full of holes
A doily
For your mind[21]

Williams later recalled that "we thought this was a chance to express ourselves, and we always naively believed that all the American public had to do is get wind of the truth, then they wouldn't react to it."[22]

Politics Behind the Scenes

After examining the humor of the Smothers Brothers, it is difficult from a modern perspective to see what was so controversial. Today, criticism of a sitting president or reference to the drug culture is a weekly event on *Saturday Night Live* or *The Daily Show*, but in the late 1960s, the satirical criticism that the Smothers Brothers tried to air on a weekly basis prompted CBS executives to rethink the renewal of *TSBCH* for the 1969–1970 season, though the network did renew the show anyway. The show's renewal leads to my third research question: Why did CBS react the way they did?

21. Used by permission of the copyright holder, Mason Williams.
22. Rebroadcast interview for E! in 1992.

What really prompted CBS to fire the Smothers Brothers after their initial renewal? In my historical analysis of the events leading up to the duo's firing, there are several factors at play that, in toto or in part, led to the Smothers Brothers' firing.

Perceived Loss of Effective Control by CBS

The perceived loss of creative control is the argument that CBS put forth in its original press releases, as well as the argument that *TV Guide* used to defend the CBS decision. However, according to an interview with Tom Smothers, the proclamation that Tom and Dick were not following the rules contradicts their original contract in which they were given complete creative control.[23] The *TV Guide* editorial could be seen as an attempt to manufacture "the appearance of consent" for CBS's actions, "in which the system's inequities are suppressed by a powerful and elaborate mythic discourse establishing fairness of democracy in the United States" (J. Lewis 1999, 255). Perhaps CBS also feared that Tom would use the program as a springboard for lobbying for new federal guidelines against corporate censorship. Of course, CBS has the right to air whatever programs it wants to air. However, the licenses granted by the federal government have the dual responsibility of protecting the American public from the most licentious of material while acting for the benefit of all. In the case of the Smothers Brothers, the material was not a threat to the moral good and served an underrepresented minority (the antiestablishment, antiwar movement) while making a profit for CBS.

Fear of Lawsuits

A week after CBS edited the March 30 episode (which was originally supposed to air on March 9), Jackie Mason sued the network for twenty million dollars, claiming that the censor had rendered

---

23. Ibid.

his monologue meaningless. Fearing that this litigation might start a trend of similar lawsuits, the network may have been prompted by accountants and legal counsel to cut its losses and drop the program.

Drop in Ratings

The theory that *TSBCH* was canceled because of a drop in ratings plays on the previous one, in that the program had dropped to as low as forty-seventh place in the Nielsen ratings, and, at a then-unheard-of cost of $375,000 per episode, the controversy caused by the program was no longer profitable. Although the program managed to attract the all-important eighteen to thirty-four year olds, the program still lost audience members from its lead-in, *The Ed Sullivan Show*. According to Ed Papazian,

> Whereas Sullivan attracted only 11% OF ALL 18-34-year-olds to a typical half-hour segment of his show, The Smothers brothers [*sic*] reached 19% of this difficult-to-woo group. At the middle of the age spectrum—among adults aged 35-to-49—the margins were closer, with Sullivan viewed by 15%, the Smothers Brothers by 17%. Beyond this point the shows' ratings reversed themselves. Significant numbers of older viewers defected after Ed Sullivan signed off, and switched channels to watch NBC's *Bonanza* rather than CBS's antiestablishment comedy show; thus in the 65-and-older groupings, Sullivan's weekly rating was an impressive 29%; *The Smothers Brothers Comedy Hour* drew only 20%. (1989, 360–61)

Tom's Growing Political Activism

Another area that concerned the CBS brass was that Tom had gone outside the network to press his case, courting Senators Edward Kennedy and Alan Cranston—action that got back to Robert Wood at the network. If that enterprise was not enough to put the kibosh on the brothers' career at the network, Tom's other politically minded actions might have. A week before the brothers were fired, Tom attended the National Association of Broadcasters annual convention in Washington, D.C., and had lobbied FCC commissioner Nicholas Johnson. According to Robert Metz, Frank Stanton, president of CBS, confided to a reporter that "the real reason Tommy and Dickie were axed was because they took their case to Washington" (1975, 303). Tom expanded on this idea in late April 1969, when he rented a studio in Arlington, Virginia, for a screening of the April 6 episode that he held for the press and members of Congress:

> I'll tell you what precipitated our firing. In March, Senator Pastore's communications subcommittee was holding hearings in Washington on television programming. I came to find out for myself what was going on—the only man from the creative side of television who did come. Was there any basis for the broadcasters' fear of governmental censorship, or were they just scaring themselves and trying to scare us? Had we in particular gone beyond any of the permissible boundaries? Could somebody lose his license because of us? So I talked to Nicholas Johnson and other FCC commissioners, and I was told that we weren't the slightest threat to any licensee. Moreover, they wanted to encourage [*sic*] divergent viewpoints. Senator Hartke and other legislators told me the same thing, and now there's this letter from Senator Pastore. What I found out, and what I've been saying every chance I get, is that the real pressure is not from the Government but from the sponsors and from the networks themselves. CBS didn't like my revealing that one bit, and so far as I can figure it out, that's why they got rid of us. After all, we were making a lot of money for them. And I have private information that we were already all sold out for the next year. (Henthoff 1969, 28)

The Pastore Hearings

In 1969, Senator John Pastore of Rhode Island pushed for a bill that would require a prescreening of any episode that was deemed "controversial." Stanton opposed such legislation at the time on the grounds that it was the responsibility of private networks to protect the public. Ironically, the Smothers Brothers' program was the only show (up until that time) that CBS ever required to provide tapes for prescreening by its affiliates.

Additionally, a segment on the contentious April 6, 1969, episode had Dan Rowan (of rival NBC's *Laugh-In*) presenting the "flying fickle finger of fate" to Senator Pastore. With the brothers so blatantly poking fun at the powerful senator and needing to back up its words, CBS looked for an easy sacrificial lamb to convince Senator Pastore that the networks could censor themselves.

Presidential Criticisms

Apparently, Stanton was a staunch Nixon supporter, recalled Ken Kragen, production coordinator for the contentious April 6, 1969, episode:

> I feel that the Nixon presidency certainly contributed to the demise of the *Smothers Brothers* show. We were very critical of the government in general even when Johnson was there, critical of the Vietnam War, and critical of all the things that American youth were critical of at that time, and the election of Nixon I think had a lot to do with it. We were told at the time, and I don't know the validity of this, but Mr. Stanton who was at the network was a very strong supporter and was constantly embarrassed by the fact that on his network there was a show that was satirizing the presidency and the vice presidency.[24]

24. Ibid.

When it was learned that sketches on *TSBCH* had had a negative impact on Johnson's decision to run for reelection in 1968, the Smothers Brothers wrote a letter of apology to the former president. Johnson's reply, however, surprised the brothers and became one of Tom's most treasured statements regarding the show: "To be genuinely funny at a time when the world is in crisis is a task that would tax the talents of a genius. And to be consistently fair when standards of fair play are constantly questioned demands the wisdom of a saint. It is part of the price of leadership in this great, free nation to be the target of clever satirists. You have given the gift of laughter to our people. May we never grow so somber or self-important that we fail to appreciate the humor in our lives" (R. Lewis 1969, 185). Despite Johnson's positive reaction to the brothers' apology, which seemed to encourage satirical criticism of the president, Stanton and Wood may have felt obliged to remove the program for political reasons to prevent Nixon from becoming a regular target of the Smothers Brothers, rather than over the "question of taste" that Wood cited to the media, as Nixon sketches were appearing toward the end of the third season.

The Lawsuit and Its Aftermath

CBS eventually lost a breach-of-contract lawsuit brought by the Smothers Brothers and was ordered to pay the brothers $776,300 for the 1969–1970 contract and $1 in punitive damages. Looking at the list of possible reasons for termination, it is not difficult to see why CBS decided to fire the Smothers Brothers. However, the question of whether CBS's decision was based on keeping a vocal, liberal minority from reaching a national audience remains. Tom called this "network anticipatory censorship" in an op-ed piece he wrote for the *New York Times,* which appeared on June 29, 1969: "We tried to be relevant to a world which contains the pill and the bomb. . . . I am an artist . . . [*sic*] and I would rather be performing than preaching. But I am an American who loves his country and I want America to keep its promises. One of the most crucial of those promises was that Americans would always be able to engage each other in vigorous debate on the cardinal issues of their time. Without genuinely free television, it is unlikely that this promise can be kept" (1969, 27).

With little fanfare, the program won the Emmy for Outstanding Writing Achievement in Comedy, Variety, or Music that year, yet *TSBCH* was not be rerun for twenty-three years. In a final insult to a weekly audience that was "one of the five largest in college graduates, people under 35, high-income viewers and professional people" (19), it should be noted that the day Tom Smothers's letter appeared in the *New York Times, Hee Haw*—a lowbrow "country-and-western version of *Laugh-In*" (McNeil 1991, 337)—was regularly airing in the time slot previously occupied by *The Smothers Brothers Comedy Hour.* In the long run, the Smothers Brothers lost their battle over censorship, and *Laugh-In*, the new challenger to the network censors, took over—at least in the public's mind—where *TSBCH* left off.

Conclusion

In examining the controversies surrounding the censorship and subsequent termination of *The Smothers Brothers Comedy Hour* at CBS, it is clear that most of the censorship of the program centered on ideas that ran counter to those beliefs held by the network. Yes, there were occasional drug references and taboo words that needed to be excised in order to meet community standards as defined by the FCC; consequently, CBS had every right to remove these remarks as it saw fit. With respect to the more political humor—gun control, the civil rights movement, the draft, and the Vietnam War—CBS censored in the name of its own standards and in retrospect was clearly on the wrong side of history. Had the American public truly found these topics uninteresting—or offensive, as CBS claimed—the public would have stopped watching the program altogether, with the result being that *TSBCH* would have been canceled under the weight of its high production costs and low ratings, like all of the previous programs that had occupied the Sunday-evening slot against *Bonanza*. Yet rather than offending a majority of viewers, the program spoke to it— particularly to those Americans who felt disfranchised by an establishment that still supported the Vietnam War. The Smothers Brothers opposed both President Johnson's and President Nixon's policies, and as a result of their attempts to keep both the government and CBS's censors out of determining the content of their program, the Smothers Brothers were fired.

3 "When You Hire Richard Pryor, You Get Richard Pryor"

The Richard Pryor Show

A Richard Pryor Series?

On September 13, 1977, at 8:00 P.M. eastern time, *The Richard Pryor Show (TRPS)* aired for the first time on NBC and was perceived to be the third-place network's best chance for a hit program that fall. The innovative program introduced America to a young stable of unknown performers who would move on to greater fame—the most famous being Robin Williams, who would become a household name on *Mork & Mindy* and would later become an international film star. Also introduced on *TRPS* was Tim Reid, who would move on to *WKRP in Cincinnati* and *Simon & Simon* and eventually open the first full production film studio in Virginia; stand-up comic and actress Sandra Bernhardt; and stand-up comic and actress Marsha Warfield, who would later be featured on *Night Court* and her self-titled talk show. Also featured on the program was character actor Jeff Corey, who had been blacklisted during the 1950s, only to become a highly sought acting coach. Despite such casting, press acclaim, and promotion on the part of NBC, *TRPS* lost by a two-to-one margin to the top-rated program in the country, *Happy Days,* and was canceled after only four episodes.

For its part, NBC tried to capitalize on both Pryor's rising stardom and his controversial material. Apart from writing for programs such as *The Flip Wilson Show* and *Sanford and Son,* Pryor won an Emmy for writing for Lily Tomlin's special, *Lily,* on ABC in 1973. Between 1970 and 1977, Pryor had started to work his way back into the Hollywood mainstream, starring in a string of films, winning Grammy awards for his comedy albums, and picking up attention as a screenwriter as well. After coscripting *Blazing Saddles,* which won both box-office acclaim as well as writing awards, Pryor became a hot Hollywood commodity. He even cohosted the Oscars in March 1977. It was no wonder that NBC recognized this fact and gave him his own television special, *The Richard Pryor Special?* that aired on May 5, 1977. By August 1977, *Time* had declared that Richard Pryor was "the new black superstar" in a feature story, whereas *Newsweek* would run a similar feature of him three months later ("A New Black Superstar" 1977; see also Orth 1977). Years later, in his 1995 autobiography, *Pryor Convictions and Other Life Sentences,* Pryor highlighted his tortured lifestyle and how he felt when he discovered that he was going to have to produce a weekly series. It is obvious that this period was a very painful one for Pryor, who, despite being proud of the program, found that "the medium's limitations were as frustrating as low ratings. The show also took a tremendous toll on my health. My drugging, drinking, and relationship excesses were lethal when combined with the pressure of being a perfectionist and putting on a weekly series" (158).[1] Curiously, Pryor's account provides no detail or insight into the censorship he encountered at NBC.

Even before the May 5 special aired, NBC already had plans for a fall series, as evidenced by the release of their fall 1977 schedule

---

1. Despite the personal trauma and censorship of his work, Pryor himself uses only one page to discuss the program.

on May 3, which held a slot for an as-yet-unsigned Richard Pryor program. On May 10, Pryor signed an exclusive five-year contract to produce ten programs, do another two specials, and executive produce a third special to spotlight new talent. For this deal, Pryor was to earn $750,000 for the first year, after which he could renegotiate or cancel for the remaining four years. Other sources cite that he simply signed a $2 million deal for an exclusive five-year contract with NBC, whether he appeared or not. That same spring saw Pryor sign a second five-picture deal with Universal, as well as a multipicture deal with Warner Brothers that would have him make four films in four years. Seven years after he had been deemed persona non grata in show business for walking away from several performances—including an appearance on *The Ed Sullivan Show*—Pryor was making more money than any African American performer had ever made.

The Opening That Never Was: Episode 1

The one-minute opening of the first *TRPS* was to have featured Pryor explaining that he had not given up anything to appear on television, while the camera slowly pulls back to reveal that Pryor is nude—save for some flesh-toned makeup that conceals his genitalia. Pryor explained the joke at a press conference the day before the program premiered: "I was trying to make a statement on why I'm doing TV . . . saying that TV is like those children's dolls, there are no private parts. The opening explains what Richard Pryor has to say. It's about me" (Brown 1977, 18).

NBC countered that despite the sketch being approved in script format, it would not have allowed the segment in any time period. Jerome Stanley, vice president of NBC's West Coast broadcast standards, said, "It had nothing to do with the time element. . . . We don't do genital jokes. We don't do intercourse jokes. There are just some things we do not allow" (Brown 1977, 18). In place of the sketch, NBC agreed "to Pryor's demand that the first Richard

Pryor Show be preceded by a line delivered by a live announcer: a voice over a dark screen saying, 'The opening line of the Richard Pryor Show will not be seen—ever.'"

To say that the opening of *TRPS* was never seen on television would be incorrect; it was never aired by NBC during the run of *TRPS*. It was aired by KNXT-TV, a CBS affiliate in Los Angeles, during its early-evening news broadcast on September 12, 1977,[2] and was similarly carried by other stations around the country, so that in the end, more people probably saw the censored bit on the news than would have on his program. NBC tried to justify its position that, despite promising Pryor artistic freedom, the network had taken the proper approach: "NBC Broadcast Standards made the judgment that one sketch was inappropriate, and a brief edit was made. We think the program is terrific and that Richard Pryor is one of America's most innovative and talented performers" (O'Connor 1977, 62). Despite the press conference, the opening skit was not put back into the program. The network further defended its editing by saying it was trying to protect children who may be watching at that hour, while ignoring the fact that the network had put the notoriously blue performer's show into the Family Viewing Hour in the first place.

Pryor was furious, threatening to walk away after only two shows, much like he had walked out on casino engagements and an appearance on *The Ed Sullivan Show* years earlier. During the press conference, however, Pryor continued to rail against what he perceived as a difficult situation: "What it's about is censorship . . . and I can't work under those conditions. The sketch is important to me because I worked on it, it's about me and I'm the one they hired. If they didn't want Richard Pryor they should have gone out and gotten someone else" (Brown 1977, 18). Following the one minute of

2. The television critic said, "It was more funny than offensive" ("A Pryor Restraint" 1977, B1).

essentially dead air, Pryor is then seen in a parody of the *Star Wars* cantina as a bartender who finds nothing unusual in the strange creatures of famed makeup artist Rick Baker. As *Star Wars* was still in theaters, this skit was timely and generally inoffensive, save for a line that Pryor was able to get past the censors. When confronted with an octopus-like creature, Pryor summons the bar's bouncer to take the creature to "de back room." As Pryor mugs for the camera, he adds, "And while you're back there, why don't you get yourself some octopussy"—an obvious sexual reference.[3]

"The First Black President of the United States"

In the second major skit of the program, Pryor ventures into politics—presenting himself as the first African American president, answering questions in a press conference. At first, the questions, and the reporters, are presented and answered as they would be by "any other double-talking politician, but as the questions get increasingly racial, Pryor gets increasingly 'black' in his answers" (Shales 1977, B1). For example, an early question referring to unemployment gets a very straightforward answer:

> REPORTER: I'd like to ask you a question I'm sure the American people would like to know. Do you feel, that in the fiscal year, the unemployment rate would drop below the 5 percent level?
>
> PRESIDENT: As you know, the 5 percent level pertains mostly, if I may say, to white America. In black America, the minority situation, it's up to as high as 45 percent. And we plan to, with all our efforts, try to lower that rate to 20 percent in the black areas, and of course, it will be lower in the

---

3. Surprisingly, this spoof is one of the earliest parodies of *Star Wars* (the other contemporaneous one was the Mark Hamill appearance on *The Muppet Show*) that allowed the use of the "*Star Wars* Bar" and Baker's makeup.

white areas. Of course, we're tryin' to do this to emerge as
a United States.

Of course, Pryor's answer is somewhat exaggerated, but according to a report titled "The State of Black America," published by the National Urban League in the September 1977 edition of the *Black Scholar,* his number was not all that far from the mark. As of June 1976, the article claims, African Americans accounted for "11.4 percent of the civilian labor force; 10.7 percent of the total employment and 20.3 percent of all unemployed persons" (5). Citing the recession of 1974–1976, as well as a backlash against affirmative action programs, the National Urban League states that African Americans had little hope of narrowing the economic gap that existed between the races.

In another example that the writers of this program really had their finger on the pulse of black America (as opposed to the 90 percent of all black comedy programs that were written by whites during the 1977–1978 season), a reporter asks about a recent increase in spending on the space program:

REPORTER: Arthur Williams, *Chicago Sun-Herald.* You've just okayed a $250 million increase in our space program. What I'd like to know is, the main reason you did this so we could finally recruit black people for the space program?

PRESIDENT: I feel it's time that black people went to space. White people have been going for years, and "spacin' out" on us, as you might say. And I feel with the projects that we have in mind, we're going to send explorer ships throughout the galaxies, and no longer will they have the same type of music—Beethoven, Brahms, and Tchaikovsky— now we have a little Miles Davis and Charlie Parker, and we'll have some different kinds of things in there.[4]

4. Responding to criticism that the astronaut corps was made up of only

Pryor's response during the press conference, while playing on the stereotype of musical preferences between whites and blacks, further expresses the call from the African American community for further representation in all walks of American life.

As the press conference continues, Pryor and company delve deeper into the black experience of the early to midseventies, responding to a question of whether he thinks that former Black Panther Huey Newton is qualified to be the director of the Federal Bureau of Investigation (FBI):

> REPORTER: Ro-bert-a Davies . . . *Jet* magazine. (President salutes) Mr. President . . . on your list of candidates for director of the FBI, are you including the name of Huey Newton?
>
> PRESIDENT: Yes, I figure that Huey Newton is best qualified. He knows the "ins and outs" of the FBI if anybody knows the ins and outs. He would be an excellent director.

Newton was an interesting choice for the writers of the program to select. In his autobiography, Pryor claims to have met the former Black Panther minister of defense at a party in Oakland in 1970. Even though he was still regarded in the African American community as a leader, he had fled to Cuba in 1974 on murder

---

white men, the National Aeronautics and Space Administration (NASA) tried to remedy this situation in the mid-1970s. In its first astronaut recruitment of the post-Apollo, pre–space shuttle era, NASA's first seven months of recruitment had netted thirty-five minority applicants from a total of sixteen hundred, none of whom NASA deemed qualified. Four months after hiring Women in Motion, Inc., a government contractor headed by Nichelle Nichols (Lieutenant Uhura of *Star Trek* fame), NASA received eighty-four hundred applications, including one thousand from minorities. By June 1977, this applicant pool included the first African American astronauts, Fred Gregory, Guy Bluford, and Ronald McNair, who lost his life aboard *Challenger*. For a more detailed account of this interesting twist of fact and fiction, see Nichols's autobiography, *Beyond Uhura* (1994).

charges, returning in July 1977 to face them; however, by 1977, the Black Panther movement was on the demise.

As the press-conference skit continues, it becomes increasingly clear that President Pryor favors the black reporters. One reporter, dressed as a black militant, complete with black beret and gloves, begins his questions with street slang, chastises the white reporter sitting next to him, then gives the common Muslim greeting, "Praise be with you," to which Pryor responds, "And also with you":

REPORTER: Yo, blood. (Raises closed fist) (President looks startled) Brother Bell from *Ebony* magazine. Asalaam alaikum.

PRESIDENT: Alaikum asalaam.

REPORTER: (Turning to stunned white female reporter) Whatchew lookin' at, Snow White? (Turning back to the president) Aw, brother, about blacks in the labor force . . . I wanna know what you're gonna do about havin' more black brothers as quarterbacks in the National Football Honkey League? ("Right ons" are muttered by press corps)

PRESIDENT: I plan not only to have lots of black quarterbacks, but we're gonna have black coaches and black owners of teams. As long as there're gonna be football, there's gonna be some black in it, somewhere. Because I'm tired of this mess that's been goin' down. Ever since the Rams got rid of James Harris . . . (visibly upset)

REPORTER: (White reporter with southern accent) Mr. President?

PRESIDENT: Yeah, what?!

REPORTER: Mr. Bigby, *Mississippi Herald*—

PRESIDENT: Sit down!

There were only a handful of African American quarterbacks in the National Football League (NFL) at the time, no African American head coaches, no African American owners, and only a few African American assistant coaches. Although advances have been made over the years with respect to coaching and the position of quarterback, there are still no African American owners in the NFL today. Pryor's criticism in 1977, therefore, unfortunately still rings true today.[5]

As the press conference continues, the material begins to become not only more "black" but also more and more personal with respect to Pryor's real life:

> REPORTER: Mrs. Fenton Carlton Macker, *Christian Women's News.* Since you've become president, you've been seen and photographed in the arms of white women. ("Oohs" from the press corps) Frankly, sir, you've been courtin' an awful lot of white women. Will this continue?
>
> PRESIDENT: (Looking smug and proud) As long as I can keep it up. (Laughs) I mean, why do you think they call it the "White House"? (Laughs)

The first part of the joke is easily a double entendre with respect to his sexual prowess, and it also points to the reality that Pryor himself had dated and married white women. Culturally, however, miscegenation and interracial marriage were still taboo subjects in many parts of the South.

By the last question of the press conference, Pryor as president is visibly upset, barking at the last reporter, who struggles to ask his question:

> REPORTER: Your predecessor, you know, President Carter, well, his mother was a nurse before—
>
> PRESIDENT: What is your question about, sir?
>
> REPORTER: I'm leading up to my question—my question's about your mother— (Press corps erupts)

5. As of 2007, there were still no majority African American National Football League franchise owners.

PRESIDENT: Please, the man has a right to ask his question. Please, please. Let's have some decorum. Now, what is the question about my mother?

REPORTER: Your mother was a maid in Atlanta—

PRESIDENT: Yeah?!

REPORTER: Now, after your tenure, if your mother goes back to being a maid—(Heavy southern accent) will your mommy do my house?

PRESIDENT: Aw, sh—

As Pryor jumps off the podium to attack the reporter for his indiscrete question, the press conference ends in disaster.

The rest of the first program is a mixed bag. In a musical number, a construction worker sings "I've Got to Be Me" while he strips out of his working garb, revealing a yellow bikini, and slips into high heels. His transvestite transformation is complete as he tosses off his hard hat, a long blond wig finishing off his outfit. "It is not," wrote *New York Times* reviewer John J. O'Connor at the time, "once again, the stuff of family viewing" (1977, 62). In the next skit, Pryor plays a revival-type, backwoods faith healer named Mojo, who asks his followers to "let Mojo handle it." During the sketch, Pryor's character throws a disabled woman from her wheelchair, telling her she must learn to crawl before she can learn to walk; provides a cure for a man who claims his wife is ugly by placing a paper bag over her head; and tries to molest female conjoined twins. Tom Shales, writing for the *Washington Post* at the time, thought it was an unforgettable, "nightmarish vignette. . . . [A]s a vitriolic lampoon of pseudo-religious fervor this is not particularly funny, but it is unquestionably alarming" (1977, B1).

"Satin Doll"

Pryor closes the first program, however, in an elaborate production in which he plays a soldier returning home from World War

II. Pryor's character intends to propose to his sweetheart, who is now the featured star, "Satin Doll," at the Club Harlem. The production values are high, and Pryor allows his cast to take center stage. O'Connor wrote at the time, "This is no mere routine. It is a recreation of a period and style that is quintessentially black. The entertainment is skillfully blended with unsentimental pathos. Mr. Pryor gets invaluable help from a superbly talented multiracial cast, most notably from Paula Kelly" (1977, 62). It is interesting to note that Pryor chose to combat nostalgia for the fifties with nostalgia for the forties—as *Happy* Days and *Laverne & Shirley* were both set in the 1950s—yet still, Fonzie's Hollywood adventure easily beat Pryor's program. The program placed forty-first for the week, coming in third for the evening behind *Happy Days* and *Laverne & Shirley* and a televised baseball playoff game.

Episode 2

Whereas the opening skit of Pryor's second program was not controversial at all, the second skit of the program that aired on September 20, 1977, was typical of the explosive nature of Richard Pryor's humor, the kind that Louis Robinson of *Ebony* described at the time as being so controversial that the viewer *should* watch, remaining "perched on the edge of your seat, ready just in case Richard at any moment did something that would make it necessary for every Black person in America to suddenly drop whatever he or she was doing and run like hell!" (1978, 116)

"The Mississippi Rape Trial"

The second vignette is a parody of the rape trial in *To Kill a Mockingbird* (as well as a minor tribute to the trial scenes in *Inherit the Wind*), in which the fate of a young black man rests in the hands of a white attorney. The entire piece is filled with historic racism, as we are introduced to the proceedings by what sounds like an authentic radio newscast from the time period:

Good afternoon, this is Press Peterson, the voice of NBC Radio News, reporting to you live from the courthouse in Beauville, Mississippi. The atmosphere is intense, as Wilbert Smith, a colored man, is on trial for his life. Smith attacked a young white woman, one Oralee Dupree. The weather is sweltering on this July 15, in the year of our Lord 1926, here in Beauville. As I gaze out over this courtroom, I can see that even some of the coloreds are sweating. This trial . . . (Reporter fades)

Like most courtroom dramas, the audience gets to see various members of the courtroom audience as they prepare for the proceedings, including the blind man who enters, only to find, after sitting down, that he is on the wrong side of the aisle. He confirms this fact by touching the hair of the white man whom he is seated next to, promptly standing up and moving to the clearly marked "Colored Section." We then hear a conversation between two white women, who discuss what they will do once the correct verdict is in:

WHITE SPECTATOR 1: What are you gonna wear?

WHITE SPECTATOR 2: To what?

WHITE SPECTATOR 1: To the hangin'!

WHITE SPECTATOR 2: Oh, well that depends on whether they're takin' pictures like the last time. I always wear pink when there's photographs.

WHITE SPECTATOR 1: Well somebody's lyin'. If he had really attacked her, she would have committed suicide.

As the camera shifts back to the radio announcer, we learn that "this trial has become a battle between legal giants . . . the defense by John Brownstein, and for the prosecution, Mississippi's own Big Ed Garvey." Garvey, played by Pryor, was a new, experimental character that Pryor had created for the program, and we soon learn that Garvey is "one of the meanest white prosecutors the South has ever seen."

The judge, portrayed by veteran Jeff Corey, plays the stereotypical white judge with vigor: "Before we move on to the summations, does the defendant have anything to say? (Cut to the defendant, with the sheriff's shotgun pointed at his head. The defendant says nothing) Takin' the Fifth Amendment, huh, boy? Smart move. Will the defense attorney get on with his statement? We don't have an eternity to wait!" A young Robin Williams, in his first major role on a regular television series, plays the defense attorney, John Brownstein. He opens his summation with what can only be described as a classic Robin Williams riff:

> Thank you, Your Honor. Ladies and gentlemen—of the antebellum South—it is indeed a sorry day for the white race, and the colored species as well, when a man of my stature must come all the way down from the civilized North, just to defend this Negro. *Negro*—what a wonderful word. Derived from the Latin *negrorum,* meaning "to tote"—now, say it with me, Negro. (Courtroom doesn't chime in) How soon do we forget what the Negro has done for you. Who picked your cotton? Who tied their hair up into neat little bandanas and sang softly as they wet-nursed your little miserable children? Who taught you the meaning of "doo-dah"? Yes, how soon we forget . . . but I'm not going to let you forget. We paraded witness after witness before you, attesting to the fine, fine character of this young man. This young man who gave his weekly check to his mother. Now can you honestly believe that this young man would attack a hunk of steaming white trash like this? (No's are heard throughout the courtroom) Your Honor, the answer is no! Now, I'm not going to beg (Defendant is seen begging silently), and I'm not going to plead (Defendant is seen pleading silently). I have one last piece of evidence that I want to bring to you right now. Because on the night of the alleged attack, my client was in jail! And you

can't be in two places at once! Now, members of the jury, I want you to look inside your rational minds right now—and for some of you, that's going to be an impossible task—but I want you to look inside there, and bring back a verdict of "not guilty"! If not, you have proved to me that Darwin was wrong, and I say to you, if you can't find this man "not guilty," then let him hang!

Brownstein's claim that his client was locked away in jail at the time of the alleged rape is easily dismissed by Garvey, who confirms with the sheriff that even though the accused was locked up, he found an incriminating book in the defendant's cell, applying stereotypical and racist logic to the defense's argument:

GARVEY: Now, shariff . . . they say that this young man was not at the place where the rape took place, but they say that he was in your jail. Is that true?

SHERIFF: Yeah. Booked and incarcerated. But the attack was at night, and you know how slippery they are!

GARVEY: *Slippery* is a key word, Your Honor. Slip-er-ee! I found a book about Houdini in his cell. It's obvious he learned a little trickery from readin' that book, and let himself out of jail, performed the rape, and then let himself back in. Slip-or-ee.

Garvey continues to press his obviously weak case with testimony from the victim, Miss Dupree. He tries to milk sympathy out of both judge and jury with a description of her innocence, even though she is seen making out with a courtroom spectator:

GARVEY: When you hear out of the mouth of this dear, sweet angel of mercy, this wonderful (Miss Dupree is seen making out) flower of the South, this handsome pecan (Garvey

sees Dupree making out) ... Excuse me, would you tell
the court, in your own words, what happened to you on
the night of the twenty-third? And if this don't break your
heart, Your Honor, nothin' on God's earth will!

DUPREE: It was a beautiful evenin', the moon was full, the
frogs were croakin' on the lake—

GARVEY: The frogs were croakin'—

DUPREE: The jasmine was in full bloom. You couldn't have
picked a more perfect walk. There it was, I was out on
the road, all alone, just me and Toto! We had just eaten
porridge at the bear's house, and we were walkin' down
the road when we saw this here rabbit, and Cheshire cat,
jumped out of a tree, and then, Humpty Dumpty—

Brownstein, ever the sharp attorney, jumps at the chance to
discredit the victim-as-witness, but Garvey reacts even faster,
overlooking the fact that his victim is crazy in pursuit of a con-
viction (and certain death of the accused) by discrediting the
defense attorney:

BROWNSTEIN: Your Honor, a rabbit, a Cheshire cat, Humpty
Dumpty—

GARVEY: Your Honor, this man is obviously a master of
disguise!

BROWNSTEIN: Your Honor, the only thing that's obvious is
that this woman is ridiculous!

GARVEY: You see that, Your Honor, a man—a stranger from
the North—comes and calls our belle of the South ridiculous. Now, I beg you to bring in a verdict of guilty! There
is no other verdict—guilty, guilty, guilty!

Finally, a surprise witness jumps out of the crowd, claiming to
have been with Miss Dupree on the night in question, which leads

to a series of similar surprising confessions, and another leap in logic from Garvey:

> SURPRISE WITNESS: I can't stand it anymore! I can't let an innocent man go to the gallows! I'm the man who did it! I was with her on the night of August twenty-third! It was me!
>
> TALL JUROR: Well, I was with her too! Oh, about ten to nine!
>
> SHORT JUROR: Me too!
>
> GARVEY: What in the hell were you doin' with her? Your Honor, it's obviously a case of mass hypnosis! Why, the mere thought of him wantin' this woman has transferred through the whole community like a virus. Well, the next thing you know, I'll be sayin' I was with her, oh, about eleven, eleven-thirty!

The judge finally directs the jury to make its deliberations, which has, "given Pryor's soured view of justice," reached a verdict without any deliberation at all (Rovin 1984, 157). However, there is a surprise twist, as Brownstein objects:

> BROWNSTEIN: Your Honor, that's ridiculous, they haven't even voted yet.
>
> JURY FOREMAN: No need to—it's unanimous! We find the defendant "not guilty." (Courtroom erupts) However, Your Honor, we find this carpet-baggin', Communist Pinko, Jew-boy lawyer guilty of gettin' him off!
>
> JUDGE: (Lifting a noose) Hang him!

The subject matter for this skit, a black man on trial for the rape of a white woman, was and still is a controversial topic in the African American community. In fact, during much of the first third of the twentieth century, just the allegation of the rape of a white woman by a black man was justification for lynch mobs to act before the courts did, regardless of whether the allegations were true. Although this skit ran uncensored, it more than likely turned viewers off, sending them in search of the least-objectionable programming available.[6]

There was one element of this episode that was censored by an affiliate—a musical number that starts out with a trio of young African American men singing in front of their house. As they start their number, their dance steps are match-cut to the O'Jays on stage, singing "Work on Me." This song, which was number thirteen on the Billboard soul list, features sexual innuendo—prompting Detroit affiliate WWJ to refuse to air the entire hour.

"Egypt, 1909"

The Egypt sketch, though on the surface not very controversial, represented "a breathtaking airing of a long-simmering controversy" (Williams and Williams 1991, 122). In the sketch, Pryor plays an archaeologist in 1909, discovering an unopened tomb that could change world history:

> Look here, you know what this is? It's the "Book of Life"! In the beginning, when man of Ra on earth, the black gods did leave the spacecraft—and they walked as they named the beasts of the sea and the animals of the land, and man in his blackness did walk the earth. Medicine, they discovered time—these were all black people, get down! Wait a minute! There ain't nothin' in here about whitey! This is ours! Wait till the brothers hear this! I'm gonna get this book outta here, baby! This here's the real thing, baby! What are you doin', jack? Black people discovered the music, and brain surgery

6. For her special, *Lily,* which was cowritten by and costarred Richard Pryor in 1973, Lily Tomlin told me firsthand on December 10, 2003, that the network strategy was to move such elements to the end of a program, so that if you lost part of your audience, it did not harm your rating.

back in the year 3 B.C. Man, they was gettin' down. This is it, brother, everybody's gonna know about this. We can change the history . . . Civilization is gonna change . . . (Door is heard closing, locking Pryor's character in)

According to biographers John A. Williams and Dennis A. Williams, the sketch indicates that "the comedian, or someone on his staff, was extremely knowledgeable about black prehistory and the debates ranging around it" (1991, 122).

"Finding 'Roots'"

During the previous season, *Roots* had become the most-watched program in television history, and that kind of success had a ripple effect throughout the industry; ironically, *Roots* did not have a single African American writer and featured only one African American director (for one lone segment). Coupled with the fact that *TRPS* was one of only a handful of programs that prominently featured African American performers, Pryor decided to tap into the *Roots* phenomenon. The program features an authentic African musical dance number, which segues into a modern parody of "Roots-seekers" in the form of the "Come-from Man" sketch. As an American tour group has paid the Come-from Man upward of two thousand dollars, he informs them that they are from Cleveland or that they have white fathers.[7]

"The 'Black Death' Concert"

Episode 2 would end with an extremely controversial, and still timely, spoof of heavy-metal rock concerts, with Pryor featured

---

7. As Alex Haley, the author of *Roots*, is touted as the "father of popular genealogy," especially within the African American community, I think this sketch is, in many ways, an overlooked humorous reaction to the beginning of the modern genealogy movement.

as the lead singer and guitarist of a band called Black Death. According to an unnamed San Francisco TV columnist, Pryor was deemed a "black racist" (Orth 1977, 60). During the concert, Pryor, screaming his lyrics, throws the predominantly white audience pills, sprays them with DDT, then ultimately machine-guns the survivors of the drugs and poison. After a performance in which he "kills" his audience, Pryor triumphantly walks offstage.

Episode 3

"Technical Difficulties"

After his experience with the opening of the premiere episode, Pryor threatened to walk away from *TRPS* if NBC continued to tamper with his work. By the third episode, which aired on September 27, 1977, however, Pryor had decided to have some fun with his running battle with NBC censors, even if NBC was not upset by Pryor's harsh words. For the opening of the third episode, Pryor begins to talk to the camera, but his microphone is soon cut:

> PRYOR: Good evening, ladies and gentleman, my name is Richard Pryor—
>
> ANNOUNCER: Due to technical difficulties, we cannot continue to bring you the audio portion of *The Richard Pryor Show*. However, I'm an NBC spokesman, and I will be happy to tell you what Mr. Pryor is saying. I will now read from tonight's network-approved script:
>
> Gosh, I'm just pleased as punch to be continuing on as part of the NBC family. They truly understand me, and they've been oh so fair. After all, I'm only here to please. They only hired me to do what I do best—be humble. Later, I'll share my recipe with you for good ol' American pie. Meanwhile, I just hope to heck I haven't offended anyone. By the way, I don't mind the fact that

NBC never aired the opening of my first show. I know
they were just thinking of me. They always put me first.
And that's why, for me, they'll always be "number one."
Now that they've finally let me say what I had to say, let's
go on with the show!

The comedy, of course, comes from the juxtaposition of Pryor's actions as we hear the announcer deliver the squeaky-clean text. We
see Pryor progressively getting madder and madder, appearing
to scream at, choke, and punch an imaginary censor—Pryor vent-
ing his frustration at what he thought of the television network
censorship system. Pryor later recalled, in referring to censors,
"I think they hire people, about 6,000 of them . . . to nothing but
mess with people" (Robinson 1978, 117).

"The Dining Room"

The first skit, a pantomimed scene in a fine restaurant, was another landmark in the series. We see Pryor, eating alone, facing
Marsha Warfield, who is also eating alone. Then they glance
across the room at each other, revealing through a combination
of medium and tight close-ups passion in their eyes. As they eat,
the audience experiences "with exquisite sensuality—spaghetti,
cherries, corn on the cob, oranges, grapes, each bite accompanied
by optic suggestion, a sense of making love" (Williams and Williams 1991, 122). As Pryor becomes more and more sexually frustrated, and not having the patience to eat his grapes one by one,
he smears them across his face. Finally, in desperation, he leaps
up from his chair and runs to Warfield's table, and the two begin
kissing and embracing each other wildly. The headwaiter signals
for the waitress, who nonchalantly brings a fire hose out, which is
then turned on. This move brings the two patrons to their senses,
and they return to their respective tables as their dates arrive simultaneously, unaware of what has transpired. Until that time,

food and sexual abandon had not been linked—let alone aired—on any mainstream network television program.[8]

"A Lesbian Intrudes"

If such a display was not enough to stir controversy during the Family Viewing Hour, the "New Talent" skit would push television standards even further. The piece opens with Pryor in an outlandish outfit, pretending to play a piano while lip-synching to Little Richard's "Good Golly, Miss Molly." Then the screen turns to television snow—as if the reception has gone out—revealing a black-and-white shot of a woman in a bathrobe, and it seems that she is in some sort of therapy session. The shot feels like a hidden-camera segment, as the woman does not seem to notice or care if she is being filmed. Her conversation increasingly becomes more and more intimate, as she describes her love for another woman:

> I've fallen in love again . . . She's a woman here in the rooming house . . . She's been so been kind to me ever since I came here. She brings me things. One day she brought me this enameled coat button, with silver filigree—and another time she brought me this pencil. I was in the park last night, I was reading a book and having my dinner, and she was there. And she sat down with me and told me about her life, a harder one than mine. Everything about her—her voice, her hands—it was more than I could resist. She asked me to walk with her into the woods, and we found this small clearing among the trees and the bushes. And we—CENSORED.

Owing to the judicious cut of the censor, we are left to imagine just what it was the two lesbians did in the park, but as she continues her tale, the story takes on the tone of a lesbian rape

8. Even mainstream films stayed away from this area until 9½ *Weeks* in 1986.

scene: "Well she got up, and she grabbed the book from me, and threw it down on the ground, and she pulled me to my feet, and she walked me into the woods. To the clearing, the one I described before. And then she—CENSORED." Then she admits that the first two versions of her story are false and that she is the pursuer: "I . . . I started following her into the woods, and she looked real annoyed when she saw me following her. But I kept on walking beside her, telling her—CENSORED." Finally, the fantasy element of all three stories is broken, as we eventually hear of the desperate, unspoken, and unrequited love of this troubled lesbian: "Well . . . I like being alone. It's better that way. At least then there's none of the pretense of closeness. None of the frustration of trying to be close and finding only walls." Then, as if by magic, the television snow returns, and we see Pryor finishing "Good Golly, Miss Molly" as if nothing had happened. The lesbian monologue, played straight, was another attempt by Pryor to show some truth on television. Such truths, ranging from transsexualism to rape, existed before television, wrote Joseph Lelyveld in the *New York Times Magazine.* Lelyveld continued, noting that television was not responsible for "releasing demons in prime time. . . . [I]t's capturing them, subjecting them to its own well-established formulas," with homosexuality as a permissible target (1977, 174). These formulas were also being worked out by the emergence of *Soap,* a controversial sitcom that premiered on the ABC Network during the same season as *TRPS.*[9]

9. *Soap* featured the first regular homosexual character on television, Jodie Dallas, played by Billy Crystal, as well as sexual trysts and infidelities—an hour and a half after *TRPS* went off the air. Although the program stirred controversy long before it ever went on the air, ABC was committed to the show, and it became a hit, running for four years and inspiring a much more conventional spin-off, *Benson.*

Episode 4

When taping of the fourth episode began, the program's fate was sealed: faltering ratings had forced NBC to give up its hope of a hit, and it canceled the program after Pryor's four-program commitment. NBC had also given up on airing Pryor in the time slot, replacing the show with *The Man from Atlantis,* and moved the final program to Thursday, October 20, 1977, in a later time slot.[10] The program taping was tumultuous, ending at two in the morning. According to *New York Times Magazine* reporter Joseph Lelyveld, who was on hand to witness the event, Pryor was "no longer in the mood to compromise," with his monologue described as a "sustained sleight of comic imagination . . . concern[ing] a voodoo woman in Peoria and the tribulations of her bedraggled paramour" (1977, 174). Pryor performed for sixty-five minutes, of which the producer could salvage exactly twenty-two words—as the monologue was absolutely unusable according to the network's standards. So, understandably, the taping of Pryor's roast during the final episode—a format that had been successful for Dean Martin in a series of specials for NBC—allowed the cadre of young unknown performers to showcase their talent while faced with the demise of a program they loved.[11]

10. *The Man from Atlantis* was a short-lived science fiction series that starred Patrick Duffy in the title character, a year before he would find success on *Dallas.* Sadly, I admit to being an enthralled child who watched *The Man from Atlantis.* Even sadder was how I felt when it, too, was abruptly canceled.

11. Tim Reid, in my interview with him on January 20, 2004, said he was particularly dismayed by the demise of the show but was thankful that he had been given the opportunity to work and perform with Pryor. He would later find success and further censorship on *WKRP in Cincinnati,* the censorship ranging from the issue of his earring to an episode in which he dates the sister of Andy Travis. With respect to the earring, CBS believed that it could not have two African American males with an earring—the other was, of course, Ed Bradley of *60 Minutes.* Such were the attitudes at the networks in the late 1970s.

"The Roast"

Hosted by head writer Paul Mooney, Richard Pryor is sitting, pa-
tiently and quietly, and appears to be writing notes while each
roaster speaks. Mooney takes the opportunity to tease Richard
about his large family, as well as the "superstar" status that *Time*
had branded him with in August: "But he's always been very
funny. He was born in Peoria, where half the kids in town call
him a 'superstar' these days; the other half call him 'Daddy.'"

Meanwhile, comic actress Alegra Allison used her time at
the podium to poke fun at Richard while getting in a few political jabs as well: "I just want to say how much I appreciate being
a part of *The Richard Pryor Show*. And it's my privilege to read
the following telegrams. Some of the nicer ones that have been
sent to Richard. Here's one from President Carter. 'Just wanted
to tell you that Miss Lillian loves your show. We're putting her
in a home in the morning.' And, here's another one . . . we just
have two . . . 'Dear Richard, thank you for canceling your date
in South Africa. Especially the one with my daughter. Signed,
Ian Smith.'" Miss Lillian was, of course, the president's aging
mother, whereas Ian Smith was the white prime minister of
what was then Rhodesia (now Zimbabwe), which was fighting
a civil war.

Writer-performer Tim Reid confirmed for the television audience, for the first time, what had been announced in *TV Guide*,
as well as joked about Pryor's trouble at a recent gay-rights benefit concert:

> As it has been stated, this is the last show—yehoo! Um, I also
> have a telegram here that was sent to Richard. And I may read
> as it was given to me. It says, "Dear Richard, it's about time
> these honkeys heard the truth, brother. Yeah, see, you're a man
> who stood up, who got down, and told it like it was. Yeah, you
> know, you refused to lick the boots, and stuck to your roots,

yeah. We know where you're coming from, because, you see, you haven't forgot where you came from. Right on, brother." Signed—it was signed, "Miss Anita Bryant."[12]

The concert, held at the Hollywood Bowl to a near capacity crowd, was meant to benefit the San Francisco–based homosexual-rights organization Save Our Human Rights (SOHR). SOHR was formed to fight an antigay campaign that was brought forth by then Florida orange juice spokeswoman Anita Bryant, along with California senator John Briggs and others.

In between the performers' roasting duties, Mooney cracked jokes about Pryor's lineage, as well as the ratings: "Besides that, Richard is my main man—he's really, truly a credit to his parents, Sammy Davis, Jr and Miss Jane Pittman. Folks, the ratings weren't too high. As a matter of fact, we were beaten out by a documentary on PBS entitled *The Armadillo: Nature's Little Tank.*"

The others made jokes about his ex-wives and his dating preferences, while still others made racial jokes at his expense, all of which he took in stride:

> MARSHA WARFIELD: When I first met Richard, he was single, and, uh, we dated a little bit. At that time, I wasn't his type at all. I wasn't beautiful, I wasn't sexy, I wasn't white. . . . I hear that the honeymoon was a lot like the beginning of the opening of the first show—uh, it was exciting, stimulating, adventurous, and she wouldn't let him take his clothes off either.

12. Anita Bryant, a second runner-up in the 1959 Miss America Pageant, was the spokesperson for Florida orange juice from 1969 to 1977, when her contract was allowed to lapse owing to her involvement in overturning a Dade County ordinance that would have banned discrimination based on sexual preference. A subsequent boycott of orange juice by homosexual groups led to her dismissal by the Florida Citrus Commission.

SANDRA BERNHARDT: I have a little announcement to make
. . . Immediately following the World Series, the reunion
of Richard's ex-wives will be held in Dodger Stadium.
There's no question that Richard is a good family man . . .
He's a real family man these days, and he gives his kids
everything that he has—a flat nose and big lips! All I can
say is that Richard Pryor is his own man—call him wild,
controversial, exciting, mad, whatever—he has never sold
out. And unlike some of us, you just might simply say, he
shuffles to a beat of a different drummer.

JIMMY MARTINEZ: Everybody's into "Roots," okay. Well, I
took it upon myself, and I checked out Richard's roots, as
well as mine . . . and I found out that, at one time, both our
families were extremely close. As a matter of fact, at one
time, we owned them.

In the middle of all this joking, however, came perhaps the
best summation of the all-around experience that was *TRPS*, this
time from Robin Williams: "All I can say, though, is this man's a
genius. . . . Now who else can take all the forms of comedy—slap-
stick, satire, mime, stand-up—and turn it into something that of-
fends everyone?" The roast ended with a long monologue about
Pryor as a baseball player trying out for the Dodgers by David
Banks, one of the program's writers, as well as a dear friend.

"Titanic *Lifeboat*"

Following the roast was a skit that was based, in part, on Arthur
"Arthuro" Pfister's epic poem "Shine and the *Titanic*." The sketch
opens with Pryor in a lifeboat, searching for survivors of the sinking of the *Titanic*—but this point is where Pryor's routine takes
over from the poem. Following the first survivor, each successive
survivor calls out one racial epithet after another: "Sambo," "tar
baby," "schwatze" (German and Yiddish for "black"), "coon,"

"jigaboo," "burr head," "darky," "shinola," "Remus," and "jungle bunny." Finally, when everyone is aboard, the first survivor calls the other white survivors to task: "I just want to say one thing. I find it appalling that you called this man, who saved your lives, those names! It's appalling! It's appalling!" His distaste for their racism is short-lived, as another survivor discovers that the boat is overladen: "Great scott, man, have you taken leave of your senses? This lifeboat's sinking! One of us must leave!" The first survivor responds, "Oh, I see. Well, throw the nigger overboard then!"

Unlike the hero of Pfister's epic poem, however, Pryor's character is determined to stay on board: "You ain't throwin' this nigger nowhere! If anybody's goin', it might be the nigger-lover, but it ain't goin' to be me! I don't know nothin' about no boats, and I don't know nothin' about no water. And I ain't got no license to run this thing, but I do have somethin'. (Pulls out a revolver) This here gun! Now, I'll be in charge of who's goin' overboard. Is that understood?" Both survivors respond, "Yes!"

As the sketch ends, Pryor's character has demanded the jewelry and wallets from the survivors and asks them to sing a "white spiritual."

"Gun Shop"

Turning from racism to gun violence, the next sketch has Pryor walking into a gun shop—accidentally bumping into a character who bears a passing resemblance to the one played by Robert De-Niro in *Taxi Driver*:

> PATRON: You talkin' to me?
> PRYOR: No . . . I was lookin'—
> PATRON: Are you talkin' to me?
> PRYOR: No, I was lookin' at the gun in my—
> PATRON: You must be talkin' to me, man. Don't be talkin' to me, man—

We learn from the shop owner that the crazed patron is a "neighborhood nut," but we soon learn what may have caused his insanity, as the guns in the shop are heard in Pryor's mind. Each successive gun tells its story: a shotgun whose owner showed "law and order" to a couple of Freedom Riders; a derringer whose owner waited for a mugger to kill; a small automatic that proudly exclaims, "I've killed more than anyone in this room"; the police special that, though old, always took "care of my guys"; a revolver with a silencer that used to work for the Mob in Jersey; a pearl-handled revolver responsible for an accidental death of a child and begs to be made into a wagon; and a German Luger that spouts racial supremacy and that "people enjoy killing each other." As Pryor encounters each of these guns' stories, he becomes visibly more and more upset, until finally, shaken, he walks out of the shop. Although the sketch is a showcase for the antigun lobby, Pryor himself owned a large collection of guns; ironically, less than two months later, on January 1, 1978, Pryor would use his own .357 Magnum as he "killed the car" that his wife was trying to leave in (Reilly 1978, 46).

"Rebuttal by Santa Claus"

Pryor was allowed some latitude for his last skit, but that skit is also the most censored sketch ever aired during the program. In it, he plays Santa Claus, using the Fairness Doctrine to reply to an editorial that had presumably been aired. During this meandering monologue, in which Pryor as Santa is seen drinking whiskey from a flask, Pryor's material becomes increasingly blue in nature, as evidenced by the use of the CENSORED blackout screen eleven times. At one point, he gives a child, who wants a fire truck for Christmas, a rather unorthodox suggestion: "'Dear Santa, I love you.' Sure you do. 'Please give me a fire truck.' You know how much fire trucks cost, little Billy Johnson? Thirty-seven dollars! Your father's goin' to CENSORED. If you want to see a fire truck, burn up your house!" Santa then proceeds to describe his frustrated sexual relations with Mrs. Claus, as well as his self-prescribed remedy: "Ho ho ho! All I ever see around here is little elves . . . It's getting me dingy, you know what I mean? Night and day, little elves, creeping around . . . puttin' their clammy little hands on everything—including my wife! Me and my wife ain't been alone in 345 years, and I'm about ready, you know what I mean? So this Christmas, if your father's away, Santa's gonna play!" Santa then proceeds to hint at drug use among the reindeer, as well as himself, but given the CENSORED cards, this theory is open to interpretation: "I get a lot of requests wondering about why Rudolph's nose is red. He's a CENSORED. That's right! Myself, I'm a CENSORED. You gotta do something up here with these antelope. And them reindeer are CENSORED. How do you think they fly?!" Given Pryor's well-documented cocaine use, it might be safe to assume that he is suggesting Rudolph's nose is red because he is a "coke head."[13]

What Was Controversial

In reviewing the brief production run of *TRPS,* like the case with the Smothers Brothers, the issue is one of creative control by a performer versus a network's ability to control the content of its programs. Pryor was given such control, but because of the network's rescheduling of the program, Pryor found his content at odds with the newly established Family Viewing Hour, and his choice of topics did not, or could not, play in such an early time slot. Prior to his film work, Pryor was known as a blue entertainer whose stage act and comedy albums—though immensely

13. Pryor went underground in the early 1970s, during which time he got into cocaine quite heavily, ending with a well-publicized freebasing accident in 1980, during which he was burned over 50 percent of his body. Pryor's genius later turned this sad event into a comic routine.

popular—could not be aired on radio or broadcast television in their entirety then or now as defined by *FCC v. Pacifica Foundation* because of his explicit use of language.[14] As a professional, Pryor knew that even with creative control, he would never be allowed to air his usual repertoire of material; however, he also knew that there were major issues of race, inequality, gun control, and sexual orientation that were not being addressed on a weekly basis on broadcast television. In the end, despite positive critical reviews, a combination of poor scheduling that led to poor ratings, network affiliates refusing to air the program, and negative press over network censorship led NBC to cancel the program after only four episodes.

It Was the "Year of Richard Pryor," So What Happened?

A "Series" or a "Series of Specials"?

In May 1977, on the perceived strength of Richard Pryor's network special, NBC pursued Pryor for a network series. The struggling third-place network believed he could become a major star, saying that "once we get him on the air, the audience will recognize him as the star he is and he'll keep going and going" (Rovin 1984, 154). But at the press conference NBC held to announce its fall lineup, Pryor was confused about the details of the contract he had signed: NBC believed it had signed Pryor to a series, whereas Pryor thought he had signed on to do a series of specials. Perhaps the confusion did not come until the first contract negotiation, in which Pryor insisted that he did not want to be on during the Family Viewing Hour, nor did he want network censors tampering with his material. NBC agreed to these terms, stating that if Pryor would commit to ten one-hour programs, the shows would

14. *FCC v. Pacifica Foundation,* 438 U.S. 726 (1978).

be aired on Thursdays from nine to ten. Pryor then left for a vacation with his family, leaving the responsibility of scheduling his film and television work to his representatives.

Ten Shows Add Up to a Series, Right?

NBC, desperate for a hit program, wanted to make *Pryor* a household word. After all, NBC had retained Pryor's services more than any other network at the time: he had written for and performed on *The Flip Wilson Show,* written for *Sanford and Son,* performed on *Saturday Night Live,* hosted *The Midnight Special,* and was a regular guest on *The Tonight Show.* The network moved ahead with its plans for *TRPS,* unaware that Pryor was not really interested in becoming a household word—at least not in the way that NBC envisioned such an outcome.

Unaware of the precarious relationship between Pryor and the network, someone in charge of scheduling had a brilliant idea: Richard Pryor would attract younger viewers, viewers who would turn their dials from *Happy Days* and *Laverne & Shirley,* the two most watched programs in the country. This schedule change put *TRPS* firmly in the Family Viewing Hour, where Pryor had originally said he did not want to be and where critics mutually agreed he should not be at all. Neither did Pryor, who again threatened to walk away from his contract.

Over the summer of 1977, however, Pryor found himself backed into a corner between his television and film commitments. His television writers begged him to continue, telling him he had the chance to do something different on television and reminding him that they had given up more lucrative projects in order to work with him. Despite this urging, Pryor began to speak publicly about his dissatisfaction with his contract, telling Rona Barrett of *Good Morning, America* about his troubles on August 3, causing NBC executives who "worried previously about potential censorship problems, [to] now started worrying about whether or not there would be a Richard Pryor show at all" (Haskins 1984, 144). The more Pryor refused, the more intense NBC became in its pursuit, at one point paying for a banner aircraft to fly over Pryor's house, its banner reading (à la *The Wizard of Oz*), "Surrender Richard." Fearing that their potential breakout hit would never make it to the air, NBC agreed to Pryor's request to renegotiate the terms of his contract. They had little choice, as NBC was "already touting the Pryor coup to advertisers as a sign of renewed life" (Rovin 1984, 155). The network put the best face it could on the new deal, which called for four episodes instead of ten, with Pryor holding the option to do more if he wished, plus two or three specials a year. For his part, Pryor was not convinced, but tried to remain open-minded as he pressed forward with his writing staff.

Censorship by the Network

Given that the network had gone back on its word by scheduling *TRPS* during the Family Viewing Hour on a different day in an attempt to counterprogram *Happy Days* and *Laverne & Shirley*, the program now had to meet the more stringent self-regulatory rules outlined by the two agencies for Family Viewing Hour programming, the NAB and FCC. Whereas *Roots* had broken new ground for allowing nudity on network television during its run the previous season, albeit at a later hour, the NBC standards department balked at the opening of the first program, which had Pryor in a body stocking, simulating nudity. It was a second violation of the spirit, if not the letter, of the agreement Pryor had signed with NBC that was supposed to give him creative control. After the excision of the first program's opening, Pryor held a press conference and threatened to walk away from his contract completely if NBC censors continued to tamper with his work. Pryor added that although his complaint was with the censor, "no one is willing to make a decision; everybody is afraid to take a step. We showed the program to the executives and all the executives loved it. Then the censors come along. They have a ludicrous idea of what is good taste and what is bad taste" ("A Pryor Restraint" 1977, B1). Pryor did not quit entirely, but did announce the following ultimatum concerning censorship: "If it's not resolved, if we can't find a reasonable means of dealing with it, then Tuesday night's (taping) probably will be the last. Everybody will say I'm crazy if I quit, that I'll be the crazy nigger who ran off from NBC, but this is stifling my creativity and I just can't work under those conditions" (B1). After a meeting with NBC network president Robert Mulholland, in which the executive admitted that the censorship system was imperfect, Pryor agreed to continue with the show.

Censorship by Network Affiliates

Further hampering the success of *TRPS* were the network's affiliates, many of which refused to air the program outright, a move that is tolerated under most network agreements if the local affiliate deems the material inappropriate for local viewers. For example, the NBC affiliates in Grand Rapids, Michigan, and Winston-Salem, North Carolina, refused to air the premiere episode, whereas stations in Boston and Philadelphia agreed to air the program only at 11:30 on Sunday nights. The third episode, which included the lesbian sketch, was deemed offensive by the Detroit affiliate, which decided to run the program the following Sunday evening. Many other stations, according to NBC publicist Kathi Fearn-Banks, did not carry the program at all, further hurting ratings.[15]

15. This point is noted by Jim Haskins (1984), whose source was Kathi Fearn-Banks. The fact that many affiliates chose not to carry the program was not widely reported at the time.

Negative Press, Homosexuals, and the Fund-raiser

Even though Pryor worked hard to dispel his reputation as un-reliable and unpredictable, he could create a firestorm of contro-versy at any moment, a part of what Maureen Orth calls his "aura of danger" (1977, 60). An example of this negative press took place after comments he made during a stand-up routine at a fund-raiser for gay and lesbian rights titled "A Star-Spangled Night for Rights: A Celebration for Human Rights."

Asked to appear at the event by his friend Lily Tomlin, Pryor went in support of the event. By the time he went onstage, he was outraged by what he had witnessed backstage. During his routine, Pryor launched into a tirade over what he believed was discrimi-nation against an all-black dance group known as the Lockers:

> I came here for human rights, but I am seeing what it's really about. Fags are prejudiced. I see the four niggahs you have dispersed. White folks are having good fun here tonight. The Locker Dancers came back stage dripping with sweat but all you could say is "Oh that was nice." But when the ballet danc-ers came out dancing to that funny music you said, "Wow, those are some bad mothers." Anita's [Bryant] getting over. How can fags be racists? I thought since this was a night for human rights, there'd be some human being here. . . . This is an evening about human rights, and I'm a human being. I just wanted to see where you was really at, and I wanted to test you to your motherfucking soul. I'm doing this shit for nut-hin'. But I wanted to come here and tell you to kiss my ass . . . with your bullshit. You understand? When the niggers were burnin' down Watts, you motherfuckers was doin' what you wanted to do on Hollywood Boulevard! (Kisner 1977, 55–56)

Pryor had been drinking heavily that evening and went on-stage unprepared. Recalling the incident, Pryor would later tell

Jim Cleaver of the *Los Angeles Sentinel,* "When a white dance act went on stage, every damn body and his brother went to fix the lights. They didn't do shit for the Lockers. . . . Then a fire marshal started to reprimand a black youngster, and the white folks simply turned their backs and ignored what was going on and I got mad as hell" (Haskins 1984, 149). Before Pryor left the stage, he added, "You can all kiss my happy, rich black ass" (150).[16]

Despite the positive spin put on the incident by *Jet* reporter Ronald Kisner, who claimed that the evening belonged to Pryor, negative publicity from Pryor's comments poured in, and there was some speculation that it would have an impact on his career. Universal Pictures, afraid of the negative press, wondered if it might impact the impending release of Pryor's latest film, *Which Way Is Up?* Several gay actors later placed an ad protesting his benefit performance in *Variety,* claiming that they were outraged by Pryor's remarks, but that because they were not rich, it had taken them some time to collect the money for the ad (Rovin 1984).

The worst backlash came that October, when the gay-activist group YOU, Unlimited presented, in a mock ceremony, $120 scholarships to the three individuals it believed had done the most harm to gay causes: Anita Bryant, Senator John Briggs, and Richard Pryor. Other reports that followed speculated that Lily Tomlin would not appear with Pryor in Universal Studios' *Sting II,* that NBC was going to cancel *TRPS,* and that homosexual groups were planning to boycott his records and movies; however, none of these threats materialized.[17] Although some believed that Pryor

16. Comedian and singer Bette Midler, shocked by Pryor's behavior, ad-libbed that the audience was free to kiss her white ass, and the show moved forward.

17. The film *The Sting II* was not made for another six years, and neither Tomlin nor Pryor appeared in the film—that dubious honor went to Jackie Gleason and Mac Davis. However, Pryor did appear in *The Toy* with Gleason in 1982.

had "committed the sin, often fatal, of offending one of the most powerful groups in entertainment and arts" (Williams and Williams 1991, 119), Steve Krantz, the Universal Pictures producer for *Which Way Is Up?* said, "The people in the rest of the country don't give a damn about his attitude toward gays." Tomlin insisted that she and Pryor were still friends, stating, "When you hire Richard Pryor, you get Richard Pryor" (Orth 1977, 60).[18] NBC did not cancel the program, and the proposed boycott never materialized.

Only Twenty Million Viewers?

A few weeks later, citing poor ratings, NBC canceled *TRPS*, and the remaining specials under Pryor's contract were never made. NBC paid off the remainder of Pryor's two million–dollar contract in exchange for his commitment not to appear on any other network for the duration of the contract. For NBC's part of the fiasco, to paraphrase Lily Tomlin, it hired Richard Pryor and was then surprised when it got Richard Pryor: "When a network says it wants Richard Pryor, it apparently means it wants Richard Pryor's good and exploitable name without also accepting the special combustible qualities that made him valued and popular in the first place" ("A Pryor Restraint" 1977, B1). The irony of this situation was immediately apparent to anyone who read page L63 of the *New York Times* on the day the show premiered. In the upper-left-hand corner of the page is a small two-column article reporting Pryor's press conference and the censorship he had experienced upon the opening of the first show, while next to it is a quarter-page advertisement for the very same episode of *The Richard Pryor Show.* The ad shows a wildly gesticulating, premustached Pryor, and the large, bold copy seen above his head takes the form of censored comic-strip language:

18. Lily Tomlin reasserted this phrase, as well as her friendship with Pryor, to me in a phone interview on December 10, 2003.

!!#"*

AND!#**

"%?!!#

!!#*"?!*"

Conclusion

It is obvious from the print ad (which ran nationwide) that NBC believed Richard Pryor was simply a foulmouthed comic who could be tamed by its "CENSORED" cards. What the network got instead was a comic virtuoso with an agenda to challenge the establishment through the use of humor on issues of race, gun control, and sexuality. Months after the cancellation of the program, Pryor spoke of his idea of what television could become: "It could be such an informative medium. One week of truth on TV could just straighten out everything. One hundred and twenty-seven million people watch television every night; that's why they use it to sell stuff. They've misused it a long time so now it's just a business, that's all. It's just a place where you sell products and they sell their kind of information the way they want to sell it to perpetuate their businesses. They're not going to write shows about how to revolutionize America" (Robinson 1978, 117–18). For Richard Pryor, NBC's mismanagement of the situation resulted in a missed opportunity to change the television landscape with his art. If left unfettered by network censors and given a more appropriate time slot, Richard Pryor might have stayed on television, and NBC might have had the breakout hit it so desperately needed in 1977.

4 Two Networks, One Emmy, and the Same Outcome

TV Nation

A Maverick Muckraker Goes on the Air

Like Richard Pryor, whose onstage persona and material made him an unlikely candidate for his own television series in the 1970s, the idea of documentary filmmaker Michael Moore hosting his own television show—devoted in part to taking on corporate America every week—seemed an implausible idea in the corporate-media oligopoly of the 1990s. But that concept is precisely what occurred on July 19, 1994, at 8:00 P.M. eastern time, when *TV Nation* aired for the first time on NBC as a summer replacement series.

At the time, the show's host and producer, Michael Moore, was best known for his 1989 documentary film *Roger & Me.* In the film, Moore pursues the chairman of General Motors (GM), Roger Smith, for three years in an effort to get Smith to acknowledge the devastating effect of GM's layoffs on Flint, Michigan, while portraying Smith as a white-collar criminal similar to former FCC chairman Nicholas Johnson's definition in his 1970 text, *How to Talk Back to Your Television Set:* "The 'white-collar' criminal is the broker who distributes fraudulent securities, the builder who deliberately uses defective material, the corporation executive who conspires to fix prices, the legislator who peddles

99

his influence and vote for private gain, or the banker who misappropriates funds" (88).[1] Although television has a long and well-documented apprehension of presenting white-collar crime for fear of antagonizing the medium's advertisers and owners, Warner Brothers (who had distributed his film) wanted Moore to produce a television program similar in theme to *Roger & Me* following the phenomenal success of the film, but Moore turned it down in 1990.

Owing to corporate mergers and buyouts, by the early 1990s television news stories about white-collar crime were rare on the three major networks, and completely nonexistent on the fourth, as Fox Television aired neither national news nor any newsmagazines at that time. NBC regularly suppressed stories that shed negative light on the nuclear-power industry after it was purchased by General Electric, CBS killed a *60 Minutes* story about the tobacco industry because Brown and Williamson was a major stockholder, and Disney-owned ABC regularly killed negative stories about Disney ventures or positive stories about rival companies. According to his 1998 book coauthored with Kathleen Glynn, *Adventures in a TV Nation*, Moore responded to a Warner Brothers' 1990 offer to develop a television series with, "TV? Who wants to do TV?" (2). However, by late 1992, Moore had had a change of heart. In November 1992, after several unsuccessful attempts to sell his script *Canadian Bacon* to the major studios, Moore received a phone call from NBC while he was visiting Hollywood.[2] Even while setting up a pitch meeting

---

1. Nicholas Johnson was the FCC chairman that Tommy Smothers spoke with before he and his brother were fired from CBS in 1969, as detailed in Chapter 2.

2. Curiously, *Canadian Bacon* is a fictional film of Moore's response to the end of the cold war, with a plot similar to the much more successful *Wag the Dog*. Both films deal with unpopular presidents who declare war to shift public opinion; Moore's version uses Canada as the target.

with NBC, he told the network, "I don't think you'll want to do what I'd want to do" (Brennan 1994, Y7). Moore also told James Ryan of BPI Entertainment News Wire in 1994 that "he had always dreamed of having his own television show but never approached any of the networks with ideas figuring they would dismiss him outright" (1994, para. 4). NBC reassured Moore by telling him not to censor himself.

With his agent and a representative of Sony's Columbia TriStar in tow, Moore ended up pitching his concept to Warren Littlefield, president of NBC Entertainment:

> It would be a cross between *60 Minutes* and Fidel Castro on laughing gas. . . . The show would be the most liberal thing ever seen on TV. In fact, it would go beyond "liberals" because liberals are a bunch of wimps and haven't gotten us anything. This show would boldly go where no one has gone before. . . . The correspondents would look like shit. I mean, they'd look as if they were either on their way to Betty Ford or had just spent a year working at Taco Bell—or both. (Moore and Glynn 1998, 4)

In Moore's mind, he thought that his vision for a show would not be compatible with a corporate network, as he continued his pitch: "Each week we'll pick one of our advertisers and go after them like a barracuda. They won't know what hit them. Then we'll go after organized religion, starting with our fellow Catholics. I've got one idea where I'll go to confession in twenty different churches and confess the same exact sin and see who gives out the harshest penances. We'll run the results and call it 'A Consumers Guide to the Confessional.'" Instead of killing the concept, Littlefield started to laugh, exclaiming, "That's the funniest idea I've ever heard. Genius!" (5). After fifteen minutes, Moore walked out with a green light for a pilot and a budget of one million dollars.

Both Funny and Important:
The Birth of the Pilot Episode

In filming the pilot episode, Moore was still convinced that the show would never see the light of day, but proceeded with a mixture of the controversial and the absurd, as the following list of pilot-episode topics shows:

> Is it easier for a convicted white murder or an award-winning black actor to get a taxi in New York City? Let's fire everyone on the show and move it to Mexico to take advantage of the North American Free Trade Agreement (NAFTA). Let's buy a home in newly reopened Love Canal. Appleton, Minnesota: They built a prison to revitalize their economy but can't find any prisoners. Mike travels to the former USSR to find the missile they had pointed at his hometown during the Cold War. And, Mike's idea about going to confession. (8)

Moore also kept the idea from his pitch meeting about hiring correspondents who were not usually on television: filmmaker Rusty Cundieff, who had written and directed the rap satire *Fear of a Black Hat; Late Night with David Letterman* cocreator and writer Merrill Markoe; and comic Janeane Garofalo. By the time taping began, Moore had second thoughts about the confession piece, and the network axed two short segments. One of them was to be titled "The Corporate Minute," and his first choice was Dow Chemical. In it, Moore and company take on the much litigated company that has been sued for environmental pollution, women's health problems, and the use of Agent Orange in Vietnam. Both NBC and TriStar thought that the segment looked too much like a real commercial, and the segment was not approved. The second segment that was cut by the network was "Lie of the Week," which was to feature a voice-activated lie detector attached to a TV set while monitoring the *NBC Nightly News*. Once the pilot was finished, Moore presented it to NBC in Los Angeles, and although everyone in the room liked the program, they were unsure if they could sell any advertising for it. The executives ordered a focus-group viewing, which gave the program its highest marks. However, NBC was unsatisfied with these results, so it tested the program in Scranton, Pennsylvania, where it outscored all other pilots that season. Such tests, though, were too little, too late: NBC had no room left in its fall schedule for *TVN*.

Turned away by the network, Moore went back to trying to produce his script *Canadian Bacon*. With the pilot of *TVN* in hand, Moore used it to promote the movie script. The tape lured both John Candy and Alan Alda to the project, and almost immediately the funding became available, and filming began in the fall of 1993. Then the head of the British Broadcasting Corporation (BBC)–2, Michael Jackson, picked up a copy of *TV Guide* and noted that Michael Moore had made a pilot for NBC. With the BBC interested in purchasing the program from TriStar and NBC, NBC's Eric Tannenbaum called Moore with the prospect of making *TVN* a summer replacement series. As part of the deal, the BBC would pick up a significant portion of the production costs in exchange for the rights to air the program concurrently with NBC.

From the beginning, television critics—who were shown a preview of the pilot episode—hailed *TVN*: "The charm of 'TV Nation' is the way Mr. Moore champions the little guy, the underdog, fighting to make sense of a vast and often incomprehensible world. Deft and understated, 'TV Nation' may become that rarest of species, a television program both funny and important" (Goldberg 1994, A10). Ray Loynd noted that "in style and content it's not remotely like any other magazine series, although it's edited like one. . . . Pray that this production not only survives the summer but makes the fall schedule" (1994, 25). Frazier Moore added, "It's the freshest, most wickedly funny probing magazine since *60 Minutes* started ticking" (1994, para. 2).

Even Josef Adalian, the reviewer for the conservative *Washington Times*, agreed: "Despite its political point of view, best described as anti-establishment-bordering-on-socialist," Moore is up front with his point of view: "Unlike shows such as '60 Minutes' or 'Dateline NBC,' which feign objectivity, 'TV Nation' never pretends for one moment that it's unbiased or rational or even fair. It's left-wing propaganda, and proud of it. . . . 'TV Nation' is a sharp, hysterically funny satire of people and institutions just asking to be satirized. You may disagree with everything Mr. Moore has to say—but you'll laugh yourself into a coma watching him say it" (1994, C15). John J. O'Connor, writing for the *New York Times*, concurred, noting that "Mr. Moore has his liberal biases tattooed on his arm. . . . Let's hope 'TV Nation' stays around for a while" (1994, C15).

NBC Episode 1

"NAFTA"

Perhaps one of the more controversial segments of *TVN*'s entire run aired during the initial showing of the pilot on July 19, 1994. Moore set the tone for the entire program with the first segment, simply titled "NAFTA," in which he proposes that the newly signed treaty will allow him to reduce costs for *TVN*. The segment features Moore's travels to Mexico to take advantage of the new trade agreement by hiring Mexican workers to replace his American staff. Despite his *Roger & Me* fame, what surprises Moore the most is that several American factory managers show him around and are willing to talk to him. In several interviews at the time, Moore tried to explain this phenomenon: "Even in Russia and Mexico, even if they've seen *Roger & Me*, they're still not afraid. I do not have an explanation for it. Why do people still talk to Mike Wallace after 25 years? Why do people go on *Geraldo* and tell the most embarrassing things about their lives?" (James

Ryan 1994, para. 7). "People know who I am and they still talk to me. There's something about being on TV and in the movies that's attractive to everybody" (Brennan 1994, Y7). While there, he tries in vain to visit the General Electric (GE) plant to see how his corporate boss operates south of the border, the first of several attempts to embarrass NBC's corporate owner.

Describing this segment to Patricia Brennan of the *Washington Post* as one he felt particularly strongly about, Moore reflected on his overall philosophy for *TVN:* "[This show] isn't out to get the individual, unlike other magazine shows. To me, that is the easy and cheap thing to do. That plant manager in Mexico, he's not really what I'm there for. I'm after the larger fish to fry here. I'm after a larger issue, NAFTA, which is about corporate America throwing people out of work" (Y7).

NBC Episode 2

"CEO Challenge"

Not content with chasing General Motors' chief executive officer (CEO), Roger Smith, around the country, Moore continued with his attempt to hold corporations—some of which were likely advertisers on NBC—up to public scrutiny and ridicule by holding the "CEO Challenge" on the July 26, 1994, episode of *TVN.* Claiming that his aim was "to show that executives who run America's corporations often have little firsthand knowledge of their companies' products" (Levin 1994, D1), Moore challenged those individuals in power to see if they could perform the most basic tasks of their company, with the winner to receive a gold-plated putter and putting green. For example, Moore sent letters requesting the chairman of Chemical Bank to operate an automatic teller machine, the CEO of Hershey to make a candy bar, and the head of Estée Lauder to give Moore a facial. In all, more than sixty corporations turned down Moore's CEO Challenge.

Moore then returned to the tactic that he had used in *Roger & Me* in 1989: direct confrontation. In follow-up telephone calls, Moore told these companies that *TVN* would show up at their headquarters on May 26, 1994, with TV cameras to ask each chairman to perform the specific task. Moore's first stop was at International Business Machines (IBM), and while standing outside with a megaphone, he yelled, "LOUIS GERSTNER, CHAIRMAN OF IBM, COME DOWN AND FORMAT THIS COMPUTER DISK!" Although this incident played well to the cameras, Moore neglected to tell his viewing audience (as well as the readers of his fan text) one thing: according to an IBM spokesperson, Gerstner was out of the country at the time, and Moore would not reschedule. The spokesperson went on to add that Gerstner could, of course, format a disk yet did not want to do it for Moore (Clements 1994, B1).

Moore did get one positive response, albeit a surprise, given *Roger & Me,* from the CEO of an automobile manufacturer: Alex Trotman of Ford. Trotman agreed to change the oil on a Ford Explorer, which took about an hour, according to an Associated Press story, although Moore claims Trotman accomplished it in less than ten minutes (Associated Press 1994). A stunned Moore awarded Trotman the gold-plated putter and putting green, noting that Trotman had brought his own TV crew to film him, stating that Ford would play the footage at its assembly plants around the world. Trotman, according to Moore, did not fear Moore's challenge and received a great deal of publicity, goodwill, and letters from the viewing public. Moore attributes Trotman's attitude to the fact that he is Scottish, not American, and that he believes that unions are good for socially responsible companies. For example, when Johnson Controls, a parts supplier, tried to replace its striking union workers with scabs, Trotman refused to accept any parts from the company, forcing Johnson Controls to rehire its union employees.

Although Moore had found one company leader who was not afraid to accept the CEO Challenge, he still took his bullhorn to Rockefeller Plaza. He seemed to be trying to prove that NBC did not know what it was getting into when it hired him, and so his last challenge was to GE: "Jack Welch, chairman of General Electric, owner of NBC, PLEASE COME DOWN AND SCREW IN THIS LIGHTBULB!"

NBC Episode 3

"We Hire Our Own Lobbyist"

Moore decided to take on the political process in episode 3, airing on August 2, 1994, and, in his typical style, show how easy it is to get action on any given topic with a lobbyist, some gifts, and cash. In a segment titled "We Hire Our Own Lobbyist," *TVN* examines Washington lobbyists with a new twist: it would lobby Congress for its own bill to benefit ordinary people. Moore went further: "What are the chances of me as an average citizen being able to meet with a dozen to two dozen members of Congress . . . to have a face-to-face, in-the-office, shut-the-door meeting? Practically none. But what could we do if we had $5000? We just wanted to illustrate that process" (Drinkard 1994, para. 6). So, armed with five thousand dollars, as well as souvenirs to hand out that would not violate the two hundred–dollar ethics limit, Moore set about hiring a registered lobbyist and found Bill Chasey in the Yellow Pages.[3]

Moore's original idea was to get a tax break for the *TVN* staff—a "rifle-shot" amendment to the tax code—but Chasey told him that was impossible, especially for five thousand dollars. Chasey made a counterproposal: lobby Congress for a nationally recognized day. After deliberation, they determined that August

3. It should be noted that Chasey was under investigation at the time for lobbying for Libya during the Lockerbie bombing investigation, which would force Chasey to close his office two years later.

16, 1994, should be named *"TV Nation* Day." It was no small coin-cidence that August 16 was a scheduled airdate for *TVN.* Chasey then took Moore to Capitol Hill to find a sponsor for the resolu-tion and found Representative Howard Coble of North Carolina, who had recently been the target of a negative story on *Primetime Live.* Moore reassured the congressman that *TVN* did not "invade the privacy of members of Congress" (Drinkard 1994, para. 13).

On May 10, 1994, Coble and Floyd Flake of New York cospon-sored Joint Resolution 365 on the floor of the House to designate August 16, 1994, as *"TV Nation* Day." Moore noted that the lob-bying funds resulted in Coble reading "word for word the ac-tual speeches we had written for them in support of *TV Nation* Day—and C-SPAN carried it live" (Moore and Glynn 1998, 183). Although Moore had shown the country exactly how far five thou-sand dollars would go in Washington, the resolution was sent to the Committee on the Post Office and Civil Service, and according to the *Congressional Record,* no further action on the bill ever took place, and the legislation died in committee.

"Sludge"

The single most controversial segment ever to air on *TVN* was one that follows New York's human waste from its source to its final resting place. In "Sludge," correspondent Roy Sekoff follows the process as human waste is turned into sludge cake for trans-portation to Sierra Blanca, Texas, where it is used as fertilizer at the Merco Joint Venture "ranch." For its part, Merco gives the *TVN* crew the red-carpet treatment as a way of building public confidence in the use of biosolids, as the sludge cakes are known in the industry. Unknown to Merco, however, were Moore's in-tentions, revealed in a *TVN* memo that proposed "riding the shit train to Texas . . . filming whatever perverse geological features they have out there . . . sing[ing] a few cowboy songs. Drink yourself into a stupor. Cry yourself to sleep" (Dubose 1996, 21).

The finished segment shows images of the sludge being spread around the Merco ranch while upbeat, comical, and stereotypical "farm" music is heard. These images were cut together with interviews of local residents opposed to the smell that emanates from the Merco ranch, whereas Merco representative Kelly Sarber quips that the smell generated by dumping four hundred tons of sludge a day is just "the smell of money."

Although it may have come across as cheap humor, the segment then turned serious by cutting to Hugh Kaufman, an Environmental Protection Agency (EPA) whistle-blower in the hazardous site–control office. The interview was added at the insistence of Moore's production company, Columbia TriStar, to provide balance and credibility. Kaufman, most known for forcing the resignation of Reagan's EPA administrator and sending her assistant to jail, had started an investigation of Merco and gave a nine-minute interview to *TVN,* of which only fifteen seconds were shown:

> This hazardous material is not allowed to be disposed of or used for beneficial use in the state of New York, and it's not allowed to be disposed of or used for beneficial use in Texas either. So what you have is an illegal "haul and dump" operation masquerading as an environmentally beneficial project, and it's only a masquerade.
>
> The fishes off of New York are being protected, the citizens and land of New York are being protected, and the people of Texas are being poisoned. Something is rotten in Texas.

The segment in general, and the fifteen-second sound bite from Kaufman in particular, led Merco to sue Sony Entertainment Pictures, Inc. (Moore's production company), and Kaufman, accusing them of "defamatory and disparaging statements . . . made with actual malice and a reckless disregard for the truth" (Stauber and Rampton 1995, 118). Nearly two years later, a jury in Pecos, Texas, returned a favorable verdict for Merco, awarding the company $4.5 million in punitive damages against Sony and $500,000 against Kaufman, but only $1 each in actual damages. Moore was called to the witness stand for the trial. When he heard the verdict, Moore defended his position: "There was no malice here. We didn't even know Merco existed until we looked [it up] for the story. . . . This trial was about shutting the people in that town up" (Dubose 1996, 22). During the trial, the jury was not allowed to know about Kaufman's ongoing criminal investigation of Merco or the special prosecutor that he had requested Attorney General Janet Reno to appoint because of his concern that the EPA itself was obstructing justice in the case. These issues were brought up during the appeal of the case, and a federal appeals court eventually overturned the verdict in 1997.

NBC Episode 4

"Health Care Olympics"

In an August 9 segment that produced some heated debates (as well as a censored ending) at NBC, Moore decided to host a "Health Care Olympics" as a way to focus attention on the fact that in 1994, some forty million Americans had no health insurance whatsoever.[4] Additionally, while costs for insurance rose, the executives at health maintenance organizations (HMOs) were "becoming filthy rich. In 1996, the head of U.S. Healthcare pulled in nearly one billion dollars in compensation for himself. That's right, one *billion*. So is it any wonder that the U.S. places twenty-third among the nations of the world in infant mortality?" (Moore and Glynn 1998, 154). The Health Care Olympics would pit the market-driven U.S. health care industry in a three-way competition against the industry in Canada (with socialized medicine) and in Cuba (with Communist-sponsored comprehensive health care).

4. Moore revisits this issue in his 2007 film, *Sicko*.

Moore asked NBC sportscasters Bob Costas and Ahmad Rashad to do play-by-play from New York as *TVN* focused on three patients with leg injuries at three medical centers: Brevard General Hospital in Florida, Sunnybrook Health Science Center in Toronto, and Colestro General Hospital in Havana, Cuba. Like a typical sportscast, Costas and Ahmad seem to ad-lib their exchange, as if this sort of "competition" takes place every four years:

COSTAS: Good evening, everybody, I'm Bob Costas. Another exciting day as three countries were poised for the global challenge in today's lower-limb competition. Now joining me today in our *TV Nation* coverage is my longtime colleague Ahmad Rashad.

RASHAD: Thanks a lot, Bob. Now you know anytime two very strong government-based systems and one solid market-based system lock horns, excitement is always guaranteed, and today is no exception.

COSTAS: I'll say. What criteria were the judges mainly looking at?

RASHAD: Well, the ER performances were evaluated on the ADCs of health care: access, delivery, and cost.

The sportscasters go on to banter about the three patients: the American walks into the emergency room with a mild sprain, the Canadian is slightly more injured, whereas the Cuban arrives in an ambulance. Costas and Rashad provide color commentary as the American and the Canadian are triaged:

COSTAS: Back in the U.S. the patient went through triage, a way of prioritizing treatment according to severity, whereas in Cuba the patient was immediately surrounded by team activity—no triage necessary. After check-in, the patients in Canada and the U.S. were exiled to a sort of waiting-area limbo.

RASHAD: Not necessarily a bad place to be, Bob, because as
you can see, some of the players even managed to provide
care in the hallways.

COSTAS: Sure, but wasn't that ankle more vulnerable there
than if the patient would have been waiting in a cubicle
like the patient in the U.S.?

Their banter proceeds when it comes down to comparing access to and the cost for the patient in each of the countries:

RASHAD: Well, Bob, we saw the United States really struggle
when it came to access to medical care. But that's one area
in which the Americans are always at a severe disadvantage
because of the forty million citizens here who are uninsured.
Now in terms of delivery, all three countries admitted their
patients with relatively equal speed and efficiency.

COSTAS: Thankfully for Canada, waiting lists don't factor into
emergency competition. For other procedures, though, Ca-
nadians may find themselves waiting for months due to
limited budgets. Now America should be able to pick up
some ground with its superior technology and equipment.
Cuba, on the other hand, may be vulnerable in the second
half because the thirty-three-year embargo against this island nation coupled with the absence of Soviet sponsorship
has made certain medicines and basic supplies scarce.

RASHAD: But Cuba is sure to pick up a big advantage in the
cost category with no charges to the patients at all. And
Canada, well, they're also a strong contender in this category, with just about all costs covered.

In the second half of the "competition," it is revealed that
the American patient has a bad sprain, the Canadian a hairline
fracture, and the Cuban a serious fracture, resulting in an Ace
bandage, a cast, and surgery, respectively.

When it comes to comparing the costs, Costas introduces representatives from the three countries:

COSTAS: Well, the scores came in, and as we anticipated, it all came down to the big C—cost. In Cuba . . .

DOCTOR: The patient pays nothing.

COSTAS: In Canada . . .

NURSE: Fifteen dollars for the crutches he just received—that is it.

COSTAS: And in the U.S. . . . .

HOSPITAL ADMINISTRATOR: The patient will be charged $80 for an emergency room visit; foot X-ray, $137; Ace bandage, $44; X-ray of the ankle, $118; $16.90, dye used in the X-ray process; adult crutches, $46. Total charges for the service: $450.70.

In terms of all three categories, it is apparent that Cuba should be the winner, as it handled a much more complex injury at no cost to the patient, whereas the American and Canadian patients waited up to two hours to be seen. Moore's original ending for the segment would have declared Cuba the winner; however, NBC censors forced Moore to change it, reasoning that "politically there was no way we could show Cuba winning on primetime television" (Moore and Glynn 1998, 162). The producers were told to declare Canada the winner, and so the following is what viewers saw:

RASHAD: Unfortunately, it may take a while for the U.S. to make its way through the insurance obstacle, and who knows what can happen with reform, but always a solid performer, it placed third. Cuba had some really great moments and wins points for such a comprehensive medical system, but until they find a way out of economic isolation it's going to be hard to sustain the quality of their system. Cuba placed second.

COSTAS: But it was our neighbor to the north who stood strong with over twenty years of universal access. They take the lower-limb gold in '94. Yes, Team Canada, seen here waving the flag of victory as another night in the *TV Nation* Health Care Olympics comes to a close.

Moore fought the censors, arguing that such a political change was both dishonest and silly, but in the end the altered ending aired.

NBC Episode 5

"TV Nation *Day*"

Despite having the *"TV Nation* Day" bill tabled in committee (which would have declared August 16, 1994, as *"TV Nation* Day"), Moore found a town willing to hold its own nationally televised *"TV Nation* Day" parade for the August 16, 1994, broadcast. A press release issued by the Village of Fishkill, New York, announced that all municipal employees were to be given the day off for the parade and the town picnic. Moore envisioned running the show live from Fishkill in order to show the parade that featured TV-themed floats, a remote-control drill team, the Shriners, a marching band, and MTV's Karen Duffy. A nervous NBC proceeded cautiously with the live feeds, but without prior censorship or approval from the show's sponsors, McDonald's pulled its sponsorship ten minutes before *TVN* went on the air, leaving NBC scrambling to fill the empty commercial slots.

NBC Year-End Special

"Small Condoms"

The year-end special was a way for NBC to determine whether to renew *TVN* for a second season, but there were two segments NBC (and later Fox) would not air on December 28, 1994. The first segment, titled "Small Condoms," was a response to the introduction of a new condom size, "extra large."[5] In the segment, Moore sends Ben Hamper to various drugstores around New York to find small-size condoms.[6] Eventually, Hamper finds a store that carries such condoms, and Moore is convinced that it is an entertaining way of talking about condoms, particularly since (at the time) "one out of every hundred people on this planet is infected with HIV" (Moore and Glynn 1998, 197).

The response that Moore got from NBC, and then Fox, was a firm no. NBC told Moore that "if we air this we'll lose affiliates in the South . . . because you cannot conjure up the image of a small penis on network television for a full seven minutes and expect people in the South to watch it" (196). Both networks also told him that it was inappropriate to say the word *condom* so many times during the "Family Viewing Hour," and the segment never aired in the United States.

"Abortion Protestor"

The second segment that the network refused to air dealt with violent antiabortion protestors and could not have been timelier when it was censored. Titled "Abortion Protestor," the segment is about a "subculture within the anti-abortion movement that believes it is acceptable to threaten doctors who perform abortions" (Moore and Glynn 1998, 192). *TVN* sent Louis Theroux to Jackson, Mississippi, to interview Roy MacMillan, a militant antiabortion protester who harassed women outside abortion clinics. MacMillan was also one of thirty abortion opponents who had signed a petition that declared that killing to defend the unborn

5. This segment was added to *TVN: Volume 1* as a bonus feature, released on VHS in 1997 by Sony Pictures.

6. Ben Hamper was featured in Moore's *Roger & Me* as the out-of-work autoworker who tunes into the Beach Boys' "Wouldn't It Be Nice" in the middle of his panic attack.

is justifiable. That petition was circulated by Paul J. Hill, who was later convicted of two killings outside a Pensacola, Florida, abortion clinic. During the interview, the following exchange takes place between Theroux and MacMillan:

THEROUX: What if you just shot an abortion doctor?

MACMILLAN: I think you should do it in love, and to cause instant death.

THEROUX: What if it was an abortion doctor who was a woman, and she was pregnant?

MACMILLAN: If you had to sacrifice an innocent to save many, it would be all right.

THEROUX: What about women who have abortions?

MACMILLAN: They should be punished and executed.

THEROUX: What about President Clinton?

MACMILLAN: I think he's probably in harm's way by acknowledging and endorsing the killing. . . . [I]t would probably to me be more justifiable to, uh, assassinate the Supreme Court judges. (Biddle 1995, 45)

Moore notes that it is a felony to issue a real or implied threat against a sitting president and thought the Secret Service would arrest MacMillan after the show aired. But the segment was never aired in the United States.

NBC initially gave Moore a green light for the segment, despite its worries about the controversial nature of the interview, but ultimately pulled it because the network could not get any sponsors. Two days after the year-end special aired, abortion opponent John Salvi walked into a Brookline, Massachusetts, abortion clinic and killed two employees, injuring five others. Moore wondered whether Salvi would have done so had the segment aired: "Who knows what would have happened next? I honestly felt that had the piece aired, had one of the leaders of this movement been arrested the next day, and there would have been headlines all over the country. Perhaps. Who knows? Maybe there could have been some deterrent. Maybe not" (45). Moore offered the piece to *Dateline NBC*, which passed on it, as the producers thought it was not appropriate for their newsmagazine. According to Moore, the Secret Service then demanded a copy of the tape, but he refused to turn it over, claiming, "We are not in the business of gathering evidence for the police and did not provide the segment to them. If we didn't have a broadcasting system where advertisers have the power to get a piece killed, the Secret Police would already have their own copy, compliments of the VCR" (194). The Secret Service then asked the BBC to provide a copy, and it cooperated.

NBC Bows Out while Fox Steps In

Even though the *TV Nation Year-End Special* finished third in its time slot with a strong 11 share, Moore claimed that NBC chose not to renew the program. According to J. Max Robbins of *Variety*, this reasoning was not entirely the case, as Moore would have preferred to stay with NBC because of "the wider distribution that NBC enjoys" (1995, 25). However, it was Columbia TriStar who sunk the renewal, because NBC would have had Moore making short films for Jay Leno and Conan O'Brien, and would have insisted that he sign a noncompete clause—all of which ran counter to his deal with TriStar (25). With that, Moore signed up with Fox for a second summer run of new segments starting July 21, 1995.

Fox Episode 1

Invading the Beach at Greenwich, Connecticut

In response to a number of communities around the country that were restricting access to public amenities, and to highlight the growing gap between the haves and have-nots, *TVN* found a newspaper story about Brenden Leydon, a Rutgers University law student and resident of Stamford, Connecticut, who went for a jog along Long Island Sound, crossing into Greenwich. As Leydon jogged onto the Greenwich beach, he was stopped by a guard asking for his resident's beach card and was told that only those individuals with such cards could use the beach. Leydon asked if the beach was private and was told that it was a public beach, but only for Greenwich residents, as a way of protecting it from outsiders. It should be noted that in 1995, the average home in Greenwich sold for $1.1 million, and restricting beach access to "residents only" was one way for the town to remain exclusive.

Leydon decided to sue the town and was issued a temporary beach pass while his case was pending; meanwhile, *TVN* was short one segment, and with four days to prep picked up on Leydon's account to plan an invasion of Greenwich's beach. The segment, "Invading the Beach at Greenwich, Connecticut," was put together in seventy-two hours, during which the segment's producers arranged for boats, planes, and helicopters, as well as off-duty New York City police divers to make sure no one drowned. Then TriStar, Moore's production company, told Moore and his crew that they could not proceed, as it would involve breaking the law—to which Moore countered, "It's not the 'law,' it's the law of Greenwich, Connecticut" (Moore and Glynn 1998, 25). Turning to public-trust doctrine that says the federal government owns the water, Moore's attorney suggested that as long as the *TVN* crew stayed below the high-tide mark in the water, technically they would not break the law.

Comic Janeane Garofalo signed on as the correspondent, and she and a busload of people from New York City tried to enter the beach parking lot, where they were turned away. They then rode to a local marina to board a small armada of boats for the invasion. Flying the *TV Nation* flag on the bow of the lead boat, Garofalo was seen leading "the hoards" approaching the beach. Within a half mile of the beach, the boats were stopped by local police, who threatened to arrest the would-be invaders, and then were boarded by the Coast Guard. Told that they could not take the boats any closer to shore, Garofalo asked, "Would it be OK if we swam to shore?" The police told them they could swim in the water but could not set foot on the beach, and with that permission, Garofalo and the others leaped overboard.

As the invasion got closer to shore, a *TVN* video crew (which had arranged for special permits to be on the beach) recorded the angry residents, who shouted and booed at the people who had just swum a half mile in protest. In an angry exchange, a resident screams, "If you like it so much here, why don't you buy property and then you can use the beach!" Garofalo responds, "Well, with such a friendly attitude like that, I can't wait to move here!"

As the residents on the beach beg the police to arrest the invaders, segment producer Joanne Doroshow escorts them along the high-tide mark to the end of the beach and then to a waiting bus for the ride back to New York City. Leydon eventually took his case all the way to the Connecticut Supreme Court, who forced Greenwich and a handful of other communities to allow for full public access on Connecticut's beaches, although to this day Greenwich is still maneuvering its pricing scheme.[7]

"Slaves"

Another story that caught the attention of *TVN* producers was that after 130 years, Mississippi was finally getting around to ratifying the Thirteenth Amendment, which banned slavery in the United

---

7. Brenden Leydon, e-mail, February 2, 2004. According to the rates published on the Town of Greenwich's Web site for the 2006 season (http://www .greenwichct.org/ParksAndRec/prParkPasses.asp), it would cost a single non-resident adult forty-seven dollars per day to park and visit the beach. Curiously, in 2007, the town *reduced* these fees to twenty-six dollars. When queried by phone on August 6, 2007, about the reductions, town officials offered, "We're just trying to accommodate everyone." When pressed if the reduction came from the Leydon case, I was offered "no comment."

States (Castaneda 1995, A10). The segment, titled "Slaves," featured *TVN* sending African American filmmaker Rusty Cundieff to Mississippi to see if he could find anyone willing to sell him slaves before the state legislature ratified the amendment.

Advertising in the *Jackson Clarion Ledger,* Moore was surprised that the newspaper actually ran the ad: "We put an ad in the Jackson newspaper that said 'Slaves Wanted.' I can't believe the paper took the ad. People called and asked why, so we said for this to work we're going to pay your families for you and you're going to sign this piece of paper that says you're ours for a week" (Walter 1995, C1). Cundieff received more than fifty applications, from which he chose six white men, giving them new slave names: Billy Bob Cundieff, Newt Bob Cundieff, Bob Bob Cundieff, Jesse Helms Bob Cundieff, Billy Bob Dole Cundieff, and Rush Bob Cundieff. The names prompted Fox's Standards and Practices Department to send Moore a "note asking if one of the slaves might be given a liberal name" (Helm 1995, E4).

While in possession of his slaves, Cundieff puts them in leg irons, has them fetch golf balls, and has them do yard work for state senator Hillman Frazier, who sponsored the ratification bill. The segment ends after the Mississippi House votes to ratify the Thirteenth Amendment on March 16, 1995 ("At Last" 1995, A1), and a reluctant Cundieff queries police about what they will do if he still possesses his slaves after ratification. As Cundieff gives each of his slaves his freedom as "Born Free" plays over the soundtrack, Newt Bob Cundieff is seen doing a cartwheel, to which Cundieff announces, "There goes one happy white boy."

Fox Episode 3

"War Reenactment Night"

For the August 11, 1995, program, Moore crafted two segments that Fox disliked, censoring portions of the first and strongly opposing

the second. Moore agreed to make the cuts to the "War Reenactment Night" segments but threatened to quit the show over "Cobb
County" (Moore and Glynn 1998). Fox capitulated and ultimately
allowed both segments to air. In the first of the "War Reenactment
Night" segments, Moore asks a group of Civil War reenactors to
stage more recent battles: "Everyone seems to have a good time
rooting for the Blue or the Gray and cheering the spectacle. Maybe
the reason this all seems like fun is that the Civil War was a long
time ago and none of us know any of the six hundred thousand
people who lost their lives" (197). So while an audience holds a
picnic, Moore has a World War II aircraft fly overhead while the
reenactors stage the bombing of Hiroshima, and then the bombing of Nagasaki, by falling down. They also reenact the then much
publicized battle between Roseanne and Tom Arnold, as well as
the fall of Saigon. Fox allowed the segment to air as long as Moore
promised to "make it clear in his narrated introduction that he, too,
thought this was sick" (Moore and Glynn 1998, 197). Fox agreed to
air the segments except for the final reenactment: the Los Angeles
riots. Shot in three parts—the Rodney King beating, the Simi Valley trial results, and the ensuing riot—the simulation made Fox's
executives very uneasy. Moore noted that "satirizing the slaughter
of a couple hundred thousand Japanese was passable, but to take
on the racial situation in Los Angeles . . . whoa! Turn off the television" (197). Fox never broadcast the Los Angeles–riot segment of
"War Reenactment Night."

"Cobb County"

The segment "Cobb County" was, in part, a response to the "Republican Revolution" of the 1994 midterm elections. In the segment, Moore decides to take a look at Newt Gingrich's district of
Cobb County, Georgia, as Gingrich had led the charge to reduce
the size of the federal government (Quill 1995, B11). During his
investigation, Moore discovered that after Arlington, Virginia

(home of the Pentagon), and Broward County, Florida (home of Cape Canaveral and NASA), Cobb County received "more federal funds than any other suburban county in the country." Moore went to Cobb County and set up an office that "would help Newt return the evil money to D.C. . . . called GOBAC—Get Government Off Our Backs" (Moore and Glynn 1998, 164). He handed out bumper stickers that read, "Get Federal $$ Out of Cobb Now!" and "If You Can Read This . . . YOU'RE TAKING TOO MUCH GOVERNMENT $$$."

Moore then has the chance to interview Speaker Gingrich before the Fourth of July parade. When asked about trying to cut government spending in Cobb County, Gingrich becomes flustered, particularly when asked by Moore about one piece of spending: "How about this seventeen thousand dollars for the Coast Guard? Where's the coast? You're landlocked here!" Gingrich ends the interview and is escorted away by his aides. Moore persists, however, and catches up with Gingrich during the parade. As Moore begins walking alongside Gingrich, the following exchange takes place:

GINGRICH: I have to warn you, there's a sharpshooter up there on the roof pointing a gun at you.

MOORE: I have no desire to die so that the Fox Network can get a forty share.

Indeed, there was a uniformed sharpshooter on the roof pointing his weapon at Moore.

Moore then talks his way into a Republican-sponsored picnic, where he is greeted by Gingrich with, "Oh, no, not you again" (168). Moore promises to leave him alone if he will do a promo for the show, which a visibly nervous Gingrich does: "No, you're not hallucinating, I'm Michael Moore, this is Newt Gingrich, and tonight on *TV Nation*, Newt and Mike save America." True to his word,

Moore leaves Gingrich alone afterward. The rest of the segment has Moore trying to convince Cobb County residents to give up their federal funds by blocking an entrance ramp to Interstate 75, trying to get Cobb County Lockheed workers to go home for a day, and trying to shut down a local library branch. Despite his efforts, no one in Cobb County wants to give up their federal funds.

Once the segment was completed, Fox executives became nervous. At the time, there was considerable interest in Gingrich's $4.5 million book deal with News Corporation–owned Harper-Collins, so Fox executives tried to kill the segment (Fallows 2003). For three weeks, Fox and Moore argued back and forth, trying to find a solution, but to no avail—Fox's final word was that the topic "was a hot potato and they didn't want to touch it" (Moore and Glynn 1998, 170). Moore's reaction: he did not show up to work for three days, then announced to Columbia TriStar that he was quitting. By that night, Fox had changed its position, and the segment was allowed to air. Soon afterward, representatives of News Corporation (which owns Fox) were testifying in front of the U.S. House Standards Committee about the book deal, claiming that Murdoch had nothing to do with the contract. Despite being cleared of any impropriety, however, Gingrich later gave up the lucrative book deal (Fallows 2003). Several months after the show had ended, the congressman from Flint, Michigan, Dale Kildee, called Moore and told him that the "Cobb County" segment had been shown to the top Democratic members of Congress: "You wouldn't believe the reaction in the room. The whole place was cheering. We have all been feeling defeated since the Republicans took over both houses. This lifted our spirits considerably. It was the first laugh we've had in a long time. Then Dick Gephardt gave an inspiring speech that it was time to pick ourselves up and get back into the fight. Thanks, guys, for doing that story" (Moore and Glynn 1998, 172).

Fox Episode 4

"Love Night"

In reaction to what Moore said was the large number of "groups that are out to harm, remove, maim, and kill those people who have a skin tone that is not white or religious belief that is not Protestant" (Moore and Glynn 1998, 14), the August 18, 1995, edition of *TVN* was billed as "Love Night." In countering the hate the *TVN* crew experienced from their targets with messages of love, the hope for Love Night was that "viewers watching our take on these people would think they were complete lunatics and would never want to be part of their movement" (15). Focusing on four aspects of hate speech, *TVN* sent the Love Night Mariachi Band and the Love Night Cheerleaders—a group of African American women from Spelman College—to interrupt a Klan rally in Cumming, Georgia; the multiracial Love Night Dancers to the Aryan World Congress in Idaho; a group of women to plant flowers at the home of the head of Operation Rescue West, an antiabortion group; and a chorus of gay men to serenade North Carolina senator Jesse Helms.

During the Klan segment of "Love Night," a mariachi band, playing "Amor," is seen walking through the crowd of Klan supporters being booed and is confronted by one man demanding that they show proof of citizenship. Meanwhile, the Spelman cheerleaders begin to cheer "Two, four, six, eight! Try love instead of hate!" as Klan members shout "Nigger!" back at them. The local police had assured the *TVN* crew that they would be protected, and as the local townspeople begin to laugh at the entire event, the Klan leaves.

Meanwhile, the multiracial Love Night Dancers begin a choreographed rendition of "Stop! In the Name of Love" across from the entrance to the Aryan Nation compound. As the music is turned up, several neo-Nazis approach the entrance to the compound, and the situation becomes tense, as the security guards that *TVN* had hired had, against Moore's wishes, brought firearms. As a skinhead head-butts the camera, the police arrive to restore order, and the Nazis give a "Sieg heil" salute to the cameras.

Then, mimicking the tactics used by groups such as Operation Rescue West, *TVN* sends a group of female volunteers to the home of the head of Operation Rescue West, but instead of harassing the occupants with death threats or assault, the women plant flowers and shrubs. The antiabortion leader is visibly upset by their actions, and at one point tramples the newly planted flowers, insults the crew with remarks about being "feminists," and goes back inside.

The fourth segment was designed to counter Senator Jesse Helms, who "has led the fight against gay rights for years. Even bills to help people with AIDS are opposed by this man, who loves to describe in graphic detail on the floor of the Senate what it is that gay men like to do" (20). *TVN* decided that a chorus of homosexual men would do the trick. The segment features the men singing "What the World Needs Now Is Love" outside the Dirksen Senate Office Building in Washington, D.C., beneath Senator Helms's office window. They are quickly told by Capitol police that they need a permit to sing on Capitol Hill, and so they head to the Arlington, Virginia, home of the senator, where they sing "On the Street Where You Live" to Helms's wife.

According to Moore, "Love Night" was a tough sell to Fox. He notes, "Love Night was one of the most difficult pieces for us to get on the air. Executives at the Fox Network feared that even mentioning these groups would give them more publicity than they deserved. Others worried that the confrontational nature of the segment would result in harassment no one wanted" (21). The real feeling, though, was that no advertiser would want to place its products near these segments, and another round of negotiations between Moore and Fox's Standards and Practices Department resulted in a green light for all but the abortion segment.

TVN also had to remove two of the five visible swastikas in the Aryan Nation segment, as well as "audibly mask one of the three times the word 'gook' is mentioned" in the Klan segment, so the viewer hears a dog bark instead (21). When the program came up two minutes short, a reluctant Fox agreed to air the antiabortion segment if it was softened and accompanied by the following disclaimer: "These extremist acts have been disavowed by the mainstream Right-to-Life Movement."

Fox Episode 5

"Crackers"

On the premiere episode of the Fox season, Moore had introduced America to "Crackers, the corporate crime–fighting chicken," becoming "the first primetime Superhero to go after the very people who might be advertising on the Superhero's show" (Moore and Glynn 1998, 47). Moore explained that just as "McGruff the Crime Dog" fought crime, "Woodsy Owl" fought polluters, and "Smokey the Bear" fought forest fires, why not have a mascot who "will, in McGruff-like fashion, apprehend alleged corporate wrongdoers each week?" (Belcher 1995, 6). So Moore put one of the show's writers, John Derevlany, in a seven-foot chicken costume, put him in the "Crimemobile" (a recreational vehicle equipped with a crime lab), and sent him on the road.

In his first appearance, Crackers goes after First Boston Bank, which had asked the City of New York for a tax break in exchange for a promise not to lay off any workers. When First Boston went ahead and broke that promise, Moore sent Crackers to ask Mayor Rudolph Giuliani why the city had not revoked the tax break. Television critic Tom Shales wrote, "Moore wants to use humor to make serious points, but in this case the seriousness and humor cancel each other out and the whole ploy becomes embarrassingly inappropriate" (1995, C1). Despite criticism that Crackers may undermine "whatever serious purpose Mr. Moore has in mind," Moore insisted that Crackers was more than just a "sophomoric stunt" (Mifflin 1995, 24). During that first episode, on July 21, Moore announces that Crackers will go on a national tour to find corporate wrongdoing and asks citizens to phone an 800 number to report such incidents. By episode 5 of the Fox season, on August 25, the "Crackers Tour" had rolled into St. Louis to a large and enthusiastic crowd.

Moore, when writing of this episode, frames it like a children's story: "At a gathering in St. Louis, Crackers received a tip about a facility in a residential area called Herculaneum, just southeast of the city. The whistleblower [*sic*] told Crackers that the townspeople felt that their community was being poisoned by the Doe Run lead factory" (Moore and Glynn 1998, 54). More than likely, the "whistle-blower" had called the 800 number, and *TVN* producers had "arranged" for that person to be in the crowd when Crackers arrived; however, regardless of how the "tip" was staged, the lead pollution from the Doe Run lead smelting operation was (and is) very real (Werner 2003).

Following Moore's established modus operandi, Crackers travels to Herculaneum, Missouri, where he is prevented from entering the factory. This point in the segment is where criticism of Crackers would be valid if, he continued to follow Moore's confrontational style and just drove away dejected. However, Crackers, as public journalist-come-criminologist, verifies the whistle-blower's story. He scoops his own soil samples in Herculaneum and has them independently tested in a lab in St. Louis. Crackers takes blood samples from children and finds their blood has unacceptably high levels of lead. He then confronts the CEO of Doe Run with these results and contacts the Missouri Department of Natural Resources. After the show aired, two class-action lawsuits were filed, and the Missouri Department of Natural Resources received nearly seven hundred letters. Despite Doe Run's claim that the company is "a leader in environmental safety,"[8] a letter from James D. Werner of the Missouri Department of Natural Resources in 2003 cited that "25 percent of children six years of age and under had elevated levels of lead in their blood" (2003, para. 1). Meanwhile, the company continues to fight the class-action lawsuits filed in St. Louis in 1995, losing a change-of-venue challenge some nine years after those lawsuits were filed ("Plaintiffs Win Venue Change" 2004).[9]

Fox Censored Segments

Following the same practice from the summer before, all domestically censored segments of the Fox version of *TVN* aired on the BBC. The two most notable segments that were cut in their entirety while Moore was at Fox were an update on the savings and loan scandal and a feature about a student who earned extra credit from a public high school for protesting at the funerals of AIDS victims.

"Savings and Loan Scandal"

In the simply titled "Savings and Loan Scandal," Moore wanted to follow up on the bailout of the savings and loan (S&L) institutions and, more specifically, find out if those individuals in charge went to jail for "their negligent, often criminal behavior [which] resulted in their customers—and the taxpayers—losing billions of dollars" (Moore and Glynn 1998, 194). Moore discovers that not only did a majority of these former banking officials serve no jail time, but they are also in fact prospering once again. These former S&L executives had even formed a support group (which *TVN* was allowed to tape), but Fox explained to Moore that the segment

---

8. See Doe Run's Web site, http://www.doerun.com (2004).

9. According to one of the plaintiff's attorneys, the change-of-venue fight had stopped the discovery process as of April 2006, and the lawsuit is still pending. On March 20, 2007, the Missouri Supreme Court ruled that the lawsuit could move forward as a class action (Leiser 2007).

would never air, claiming that the scandal was "old news" and that mentioning "former presidents Reagan and Bush would not suit their 'young adult and teen demographic'" (195). In addition, Moore's production company, Columbia TriStar, told him that it was the one segment that would not be placed on the home video of *TVN*. It was not until April 2003 that this segment was finally shown to American audiences, at the Museum of Television and Radio during its exhibit "Antagonism over the Airwaves: A Look at Controversial Television and Radio."

"Gay Bashing in Topeka"

In the segment titled "Gay Bashing in Topeka," *TVN* features the story of Sam Phelps, a high school student in Topeka, Kansas.[10] Under the direction of his grandfather, the minister of Westboro Baptist Church, and with the help of his family, Sam earns extra credit from a public high school for protesting at the funerals of people who had died of AIDS. His protests include carrying signs that read "GOD HATES FAGS" while protesting in front of anyone suspected of being homosexual—such as in front of a concert venue featuring a Barry Manilow concert.

Fox told Moore that it had already aired a gay segment with "Love Night" and that "gay issues scare advertisers away" (Moore and Glynn 1998, 196). In my telephone conversation in 2004 with Sam's mother, attorney Shirley Phelps-Roper, the family was surprised to learn that the segment had never aired domestically. Additionally, even though Moore presented the piece as "both weird and frightening" (196), Phelps-Roper said that the family did not care how it was portrayed "as long as their message got out."[11]

10. This segment is available as a bonus feature on *TVN: Volume 2*, released on VHS in 1997 by Sony Pictures.

11. I spoke with Shirley Phelps-Roper on February 9, 2004—telling her nine years after *TVN* aired that the segment had not run.

What Was Controversial

Although he never claimed to have been given "complete creative control" like the Smothers Brothers or Richard Pryor, Michael Moore was also never given much direction as to what he could or could not produce for *TVN*.[12] He was, however, hired because of the controversial nature of his work—mainly, as a corporate muckraker who told both networks up front that he might target the very companies that sponsored the program (or other programs on NBC and Fox). The two networks collectively censored or excised segments on abortion protestors, health care, the savings and loan bailout, homosexual issues, condoms, and pork-barrel spending while cashing in on Moore's controversial nature. The BBC subsidized the show, and combined with the already low production costs of a television newsmagazine, the program made a profit for all three networks. But despite positive reviews, like *TRPS*, *TVN* was canceled by both networks because of a combination of poor scheduling that led to disappointing ratings as well increasingly hostile relations between the host and his network bosses.

Canceled with an Emmy

The last episode of *TVN* aired on September 8, 1995, two days before it would win the Emmy for Outstanding Informational Series for the 1994–1995 television season. Despite the Emmy, the BBC "subsidy" that held production costs down, the thousands of letters of support, and demonstrations outside several Fox affiliates in support of the program, Fox decided not to renew the program. In responding to critics who thought than his use of humor was inappropriate, Moore told Lawrie Mifflin of the *New York Times*, "Humor can be more devastating than some formal white paper. There's no reason you can't be entertained and think at the same

---

12. In fact, he was not even given an office at NBC!

time. You can laugh, and you can think. That's my point about the top 10 shows in the Nielsen ratings: you have to do both. And people will do that. I don't have that attitude, that looking down on the American people like they're all a bunch of dopes" (1995, 24). Moore would go on to produce a similarly themed program (again with the help of the British) called *The Awful Truth* in 1999, which aired on the American cable channel Bravo for two seasons. Moore's new show became one of Bravo's flagship programs until NBC bought the channel in December 2002, at which point all mention of the program (including merchandising) was deleted from the channel's Web site.

Conclusion

In retrospect, Michael Moore was given two opportunities to find an audience on two different networks, and he failed to do so. At the same time, both networks had a marketable property that was inexpensive and did speak to a segment of the American (as well as British) viewing public. Both versions of the program ran as summer replacement series and were not part of a regular fall schedule. Because summer programming is generally written off as filler, a program must break records in order to get the attention of network programmers. However, some series (such as CBS's *Northern Exposure*) have succeeded during their summer runs and made it onto the networks' regular schedules. In the end, either network could have developed *TV Nation* into a moderate hit. With better marketing, better scheduling, its low cost to produce, and critical praise, the networks could have found a place for the program on their schedules but chose not to do so. With low ratings and pressure from advertisers and network executives, who were more concerned about protecting the status quo (and who did not enjoy seeing themselves ridiculed by Moore on a weekly basis), Moore was given his walking papers.

5 Do Not Relinquish the Right to Criticize

Politically Incorrect with Bill Maher

Loose Lips Can Sink Shows and Careers, Too

This chapter will examine the context and fallout surrounding certain comments made by talk-show host Bill Maher on the September 17, 2001, episode of his program *Politically Incorrect with Bill Maher*—comments that ultimately brought about the cancellation of the program itself. *PI* had been a moderate hit for Comedy Central from 1993 to 1996 when it made the jump to ABC at the beginning of 1997 to follow Ted Koppel's *Nightline*, at 12:05 A.M. Eastern time. The format for the program, aside from living up to its title, brought four diverse panelists together for a (usually humorous) discussion of the headlines, with Maher performing an opening monologue, then acting as moderator and provocateur. Whereas previous chapters have dealt with controversial sketches and segments of programs, this chapter deals solely with the single episode of *PI* that aired on September 17, 2001, as it was this episode that directly influenced ABC's decision not to renew its contract with Bill Maher.

In show business, it is not uncommon for a single episode or statement to bring about the downfall of a program or television personality. For example, Charles Rocket miscalculated the tolerance of his employers at NBC when he uttered the word *fuck* during a broadcast of *Saturday Night Live* in 1981 and was promptly fired. Dodger's manager Al Campanis and CBS Sports pundit Jimmy "the Greek" Snyder are remembered for being fired for racist remarks they both made, at different times, on live television. The live (and accidental?) baring of her right breast may cost Janet Jackson her career—well, at least on live, mainstream broadcast television.[1] The first four seasons of Ellen DeGeneres's program *Ellen* were eclipsed by a single episode in 1997, when real life mixed with fiction as both DeGeneres and the character she played came out of the closet to become "the first openly gay leading character on broadcast series television" (Brooks and Marsh 1999, 305) for the final season of her show, causing a great deal of stress for the censors at ABC (Friend 2001).

In the week following the September 11 attacks, extended news coverage by the major American broadcast networks of those attacks pushed each network's late-night comics off the air. When Letterman, Leno, Maher, and others did return, they were reportedly subdued and somber, reflecting the tone of the country (Keveney 2001). Maher went so far as to keep one of his four guest chairs empty to honor the memory of frequent guest Barbara Olson—a passenger on the plane that had crashed into the Pentagon—who was to have taped an appearance for the program on September 11. Yet despite this nod to Olson's memory, as well as the presence of then politically conservative guests Arianna Huffington and former Reagan aide Dinesh D'Souza, Maher's opening comments set the tone for the rest of the program, as well as the battle cry before his coming notoriety: "I do not relinquish, nor should any of you, the right to criticize, even as we support, our government. This is still a democracy,

1. Two months after the Super Bowl incident, Jackson hosted Saturday Night Live without tape-delay, or incident, on April 10, 2004. The opening skit featured Condoleeza Rice and a parody of wardrobe malfunction.

and they're still politicians." This monologue set the stage for what Maher would say later on the September 17, 2001, program, a comment that led one critic to claim that Maher had "crossed over a new—and still unclear—line" (Cuprisin 2001, B6), whereas others would note the statement as the death knell for the long-running program (Holloway 2002; Kirn 2002).

Previous Controversial Statements

Maher's comments of September 17, 2001, were not his first to spark controversy. On the October 23, 1998, broadcast, Maher made what appeared to be a disparaging remark about former president Ronald Reagan: "He ran up the debt, he lied about something much more important than sex, and he is nuts." Michael Reagan, then a Los Angeles–based radio personality, took offense at Maher's comments, feeling that it was an insult to "every person who suffers from Alzheimer's" (Joal Ryan 1998, para. 7). Reagan wrote a letter to the *New York Post* attacking Maher: "You personally took part in the venom in a way that crossed every line of taste and decency" (para. 4), and he threatened not to book guests who appeared on Maher's show until Maher issued a public apology. Maher countered that he was referring not to the former president's current medical condition but to the period of time when he was in office.

In another example of a poor choice of words, Maher drew criticism in January 2001 for "likening his pet dogs to 'retarded children' on the show," for which he later apologized (Farhi 2001, C7). In yet another gaffe, Maher called former first lady Barbara Bush a "bitch," losing the Houston ABC affiliate in the process.

A Time Line of Controversy

What follows, then, is a time line from the first broadcast following September 11, 2001, in order to see how Bill Maher's comments on *PI* on September 17, 2001, were taken out of context. This day-by-day examination follows the aftermath of Maher's comments from relative obscurity to the front page of the *New York Times* over an eleven-day period and looks at the long-term implications his comments had on the program itself.

September 17, 2001

On the set of *PI* on September 17, 2001, Maher was seated with his three guests when the televised discussion focused on the characteristics of the terrorists themselves. At one point, former Reagan presidential aide Dinesh D'Souza and Maher compare the actions of the 9/11 terrorists with those of the U.S. military:

> D'SOUZA: One of the themes we constantly hear is that the people who did this are cowards.
>
> MAHER: Not true.
>
> D'SOUZA: Not true. Look at what they did. First of all, you have a whole bunch of guys who are willing to give their life. None of 'em backed out. All of them slammed themselves into pieces of concrete.
>
> MAHER: Exactly. . . . But also, we should—we have been the cowards lobbing cruise missiles from two thousand miles away. That's cowardly. Staying in the plane when it hits the building, say what you want about it, it's not cowardly. You're right.

Maher was referring to "the United States' previous ineffectiveness in dealing with Osama Bin Laden, including launches of cruise missiles into Afghanistan in 1998" (Cooper 2001, B8). The audience rose for a standing ovation at the end of the program, and Maher claimed that he had received positive feedback on his comments by Tuesday morning as well (Armstrong 2001a, para. 8). Maher claims to be a hawk, not a dove, with relation to the war on terrorism and restates his position that the Clinton administration had acted politically—not militarily—with respect to bin Laden (Maher 2003).

September 18, 2001

In a brief article about how the networks were returning to their regular late-night talk shows, Bill Keveney described the guests and the tone of the September 17 *PI* but made no mention of the "cowardly" comments that were about to spark controversy (2001, C12). Mark Armstrong, writing for E!Online noted that the day after Maher made the comments, they "went virtually unnoticed" (2001b, para. 7).

September 20, 2001

It took three days for Maher's "cowardly" comments to surface in the national consciousness. Texas-based radio-show host Dan Patrick (not to be confused with the ESPN anchor) used Maher's comments to urge his listeners to complain to Sears and Federal Express (FedEx), advertisers on *PI*. After taking calls from consumers, both companies pulled their advertising from the program. According to Sears' spokesperson, Lee Antonio, Sears claimed that the action was not an attempt to suppress Maher: "He has the freedom to say what he wants, but we are trying to be sensitive to what is happening" (Lazare 2001, 7). Maher then issued an apology in the form of a clarification of his comments: "In no way was I intending to say, nor have I ever thought, that the men and women who defend our nation in uniform are anything but courageous and valiant, and I offer my apologies to anyone who took it wrong. My criticism was meant for politicians who, fearing public reaction, have not allowed our military to do the job they are obviously ready, willing, and able to do and who now will, I'm certain, as they always have, get it done" (Armstrong 2001a, para. 6).

September 21, 2001

ABC still stood by Maher, although Sears and FedEx had not returned to sponsor the program. Maher opened the program that night by thanking ABC for keeping the show on "without any sponsors," later amending that statement by saying that "the network did find some sponsors." ABC had, in fact, found five advertisers willing to sponsor the program at bargain rates, including two 800 numbers and a fifteen-second spot for condoms (Carter 2001).

Interestingly, a column by conservative commentator Debbie Schlussel wholeheartedly supporting Maher appeared on what is widely known as a conservative Web site, WorldNetDaily.[2] Schlussel called for an end to the attacks on Maher, claiming that such criticism was "playing into the terrorists' hands" (2001, para. 3), but this support was an isolated notion within the confines of WorldNetDaily, as shown by another of its columnists a few days later, which would lead this story to the White House Press Room and the front page of the *New York Times*.

September 22, 2001

By September 22, 2001, Maher's comments prompted several ABC affiliates across the country to pull *PI* from their lineups. In Washington, D.C., ABC affiliate WJLA dropped the program. WJLA's president and general manager, Christopher W. Pike, had responded to numerous complaints, sending the following e-mail to those viewers who had complained via the Internet: "We at WJLA were also offended by the insensitive remarks. . . . At this time of great sorrow in our nation, and our community specifically, we have tried to maintain the highest level of sensitivity

2. Debbie Schlussel is a political commentator and attorney who was a frequent guest on *PI*. WorldNetDaily was founded by Joseph Farah, who has a long association with conservatives, including Robert Mellon Scaife and Rush Limbaugh. He also cofounded the Western Journalism Center, which served as the publishing arm for the "Arkansas Project," funded by Scaife in an attempt to bring down the Clinton presidency.

in our local news coverage, on-air promotion and advertising. Although we strongly defend the right of free speech, Mr. Maher's ill-timed comments demonstrated a lack of feeling for the victims of this tragedy" (Farhi 2001, C7). Pike went on to claim that the decision to remove the program had nothing to do with the public's reaction but was a response to the lack of sensitivity shown by Maher. Ironically, by pulling the program, WJLA viewers were not able to see Maher's second apology: "In peacetime, talking about the unthinkable and batting around provocative issues and thinking outside the box is okay. . . . I feel that by doing what I have always done I kind of added to the national trauma, and I feel terrible about that. I'm sincerely sorry about it. . . . [T]his idea that I somehow made it worse fills me with remorse and regret."

Other affiliates to drop the program included ABC stations in Des Moines and Sioux City (Iowa); six Sinclair Broadcasting stations in St. Louis, Columbus (Ohio), Springfield (Massachusetts), Greensboro (North Carolina), Charleston (West Virginia), and Pensacola (Florida); and KLKN in Lincoln (Nebraska).

September 26, 2001

By Wednesday, September 26, 2001, the number of affiliates that had dropped the program had risen to twelve. Then Ari Fleischer, the White House press secretary, was pushed into the fray by conservative talk-show host and WorldNetDaily columnist Les Kinsolving, who asked about Maher's "cowardly" comments:

> KINSOLVING: As Commander-In-Chief, what was the President's reaction to television's Bill Maher, in his announcement that members of our Armed Forces who deal with missiles are cowards, while the armed terrorists who killed 6,000 unarmed are not cowards, for which Maher was briefly moved off a Washington television station?

MR. FLEISCHER: I have not discussed it with the President, one. I have—

KINSOLVING: Surely, as a—

MR. FLEISCHER: I'm getting there.

KINSOLVING: Surely as Commander, he was enraged at that, wasn't he?

MR. FLEISCHER: I'm getting there, Les.

KINSOLVING: Okay.

MR. FLEISCHER: I'm aware of the press reports about what he said. I have not seen the actual transcript of the show itself. But assuming the press reports are right, it's a terrible thing to say, and it unfortunate. And that's why—there was an earlier question about has the President said anything to people in his own party—they're reminders to all Americans that they need to watch what they say, watch what they do. This is not a time for remarks like that; there never is. (White House 2001, n.p.)[3]

Kinsolving is not a regular member of the White House Press Corps but frequently attends on a daily pass. The Bush White House has allotted twelve seats at the back of the press room for daily-pass holders, proclaiming that "the briefing room ought to be an inclusive place" (Adair 2005, para. 47).[4] Martha Joynt Kumar, a Towson University professor who studies White House press relations, describes these daily-pass holders as "colorful individuals" and the back of the press room as being "chock full of nuts" (para. 40). More recently, Kinsolving asked White House press secretary Scott McClellan about the president's position on Target banning Salvation Army bell ringers, as well as the president's

3. I have modified the official White House transcript to replace the ubiquitous "Q" with Kinsolving's name for clarity.

4. This quote is from Ari Fleischer's successor, Scott McClellan.

thoughts on California governor Arnold Schwarzenegger calling state legislators "girlie men" (para. 38). Another, more notorious, daily-pass holder was Talon.com reporter Jeff Gannon.[5]

Conservative columnist and frequent *PI* guest Arianna Huffington came to Maher's defense, urging viewers to write to ABC or sign a petition to prevent the program's cancellation. By the next day, a total of seventeen stations had dropped the program from their late-night lineups, while the controversy had boosted ratings to a six-month high of 2.8 million viewers.

September 28, 2001

Two days later, Kinsolving's question about Maher's comments—and Ari Fleischer's reaction to them—wound up on page 1 of the *New York Times* in an article about how dissent in the United States was being muted by patriotism (Carter and Barringer 2001). Owing to the unusual (and seemingly repressive) response by the White House to Maher's comments, newspapers picked up the story overseas, including the *New Zealand Herald*, which gave the story some much needed balance: "Mr. Maher is hardly the first person to make such a point. The eminent essayist Susan Sontag said exactly the same thing in a piece for the *New Yorker*, and even President Bush has indirectly criticised his predecessor's military policies, telling aides he was not interested in lobbing '$US2 million cruise missile into a $US10 empty

---

5. Jeff Gannon, a.k.a. Jeff Guckart, was backed by GOPUSA, run by Texas conservative Robert Eberle, according to Eric Boehlert (2005). He came to notoriety after President Bush picked him to ask a question at a presidential press conference. The question seemed staged ("How can you continue to work with Democrats who seem divorced from reality?") and led the mainstream press to reveal that Guckart was using an alias with the consent of the Secret Service and had at one time been an Internet-based male prostitute. Until his outing, Guckart had held a daily pass more than two hundred times. He currently operates as a Web journalist.

tent'" ("American Dissenters" 2001, para. 8). Ironically, the White House caused a minor controversy when it reportedly did not include Fleischer's comments regarding Maher in the official transcript of the press briefing, citing a "transcription error" (Carter and Barringer 2001, A1). After much prompting and criticism, the comments were added to the transcript.

The Debate over "Proper" Dissent

As September 2001 drew to a close and October began, the debate over Maher's comments was taken up on editorial pages and by commentators and newsmagazines with respect to what dissension is allowable—and acceptable—during a time of war (Alter 2001; "What's Acceptable" 2001). Helping to frame the discussion concerning Maher was Marty Kaplan of the Annenberg School of Communication at the University of Southern California, who addressed the issue on September 27, 2001, on the syndicated public radio program *Marketplace:* "We have been living for several generations now in what has loosely been called a post-modern society in which nothing really matters, nothing has meaning, reality or truth. Everything is socially constructed. Suddenly, a plane slams into the World Trade Center and people say, 'Yes, there is reality, there is truth. There are things worth fighting and dying for. There are things that have consequences.' And so suddenly, not everything is grist for entertainment" ("What's Acceptable" 2001, para. 7). Kaplan's comments, though they do not necessarily condemn Maher, seem to question whether statements similar to Maher's can have a demoralizing impact on a society that is still in mourning.

In several editorials, ranging from the *Washington Post, St. Petersburg Times,* and *USA Today* to *Advertising Age,* most in the press ultimately came to Maher's defense in the name of the First Amendment and protecting the right to dissent without fear of being labeled unpatriotic. The editors of the *Washington Post* criti-

cized the local ABC affiliate's decision to suspend the airing of
PI because of protests from both the station's viewers as well as
the White House. Focusing on Maher's "cowardly" comments, the
editorial was both pro–free speech and pro-Maher: "It is not a
show of strength to come down hard on dissent, even in times
of war. It is, rather, America's strength to encourage contrarian
viewpoints and tolerate distasteful remarks, especially when political discourse matters" ("Free Speech in Wartime" 2001, A26).
The *St. Petersburg Times* noted that although Maher's comments
may not have been the best thing for him to have said, the marketplace, not the government, is the appropriate realm for determining his viability of remaining on his national platform: "Criticism
of government or the military is still a protected right, but sometimes, as Maher has learned, the exercise of our rights can have
consequences. Maher's politically incorrect comments are a matter for his viewers, his sponsors and his network—not the censors among us" ("Politically Incorrect and Protected" 2001, D2).
Adding his to a growing number of voices, DeWayne Wickham,
in an op-ed piece for *USA Today*, pointed out the hypocrisy surrounding the efforts to pull Maher off the air in a country that
purportedly respects and demands free speech: "Maher's show is
a great example of that which distinguishes us from the fanatics
who planned and executed last week's deadly terrorist attacks.
They don't tolerate dissent. They don't believe in free speech. We,
on the other hand, do. At least that's what we say. Sadly, the over-
reaction to what Maher said suggests that a disturbing number of
us don't practice what we preach" (2001, paras. 5–7).

Even critics of Maher saw an eventual need for healthy dissent
among the country's comedians and media. Writing for *Advertising
Age*, Randall Rothenberg noted that Maher's postcomment behavior itself was hypocritical for the host of a program that purports
to be "politically incorrect," citing the need for humor to make the
unbearable bearable: "Once the horror of what the nation suffered

subsides, the U.S. and the world will be in real need of what Mr. Maher purports to, but doesn't, provide: heroic humor. Even in the best of times, good comedians—those with acuity and courage—can cast a few sharp words across the conformities, deformities and pieties of a culture and force us to laugh at them, and ourselves" (2001, 21). Though Rothenberg did not claim to be a fan of the program in general—or of Maher in particular—he lamented the lack of a strong comedic personality who could use "politically incorrect" humor "to help us work through the ironies of the moment" (21). By the end of 2001, the controversy over Maher's comments was still used as a rallying cry for the protection of civil liberties during the early days of the "War on Terror" (Alterman 2001; Lucas 2001; Vilbig 2001; Weiseltier 2001).

What Was Controversial

After careful examination of the post-9/11 controversy, it is clear that ABC, by not immediately censoring or curtailing *PI* and by standing by its star—at least in appearance—avoided the charge in the press that it was suppressing Maher's ability to be "politically incorrect." However, by not promoting the program, as Maher would later claim, by not requiring its affiliates to air the show, and by not asking Sears and Federal Express to return as advertisers, ABC essentially abandoned the program, allowing the network to stay above—and out of—the controversy. In retrospect, ABC's actions (or, rather, inactions) sent a clear message: don't go too far in expressing a political opinion on this network. The fact that the controversy actually helped *PI*'s ratings did not matter, because the show had been labeled as unpatriotic by the White House and others. In the patriotic fervor during the first months of the war on terror, high-profile advertisers never returned to sponsor *PI*. Despite *PI*'s low production cost, which ensured that the program was still earning profits by the end of its run, the program was allowed to wither after six years at the network.

The End in Site: March–June 2002

By March 2002, while the U.S. Comedy Arts Festival was giving Maher a First Amendment Award during its annual event in Aspen, Colorado, for his controversial stance, *PI*'s fate was sealed: ABC decided not to renew *PI* but allowed Maher to remain on the air until the end of his contract in June. On June 22, Maher was honored by the L.A. Press Club for his stance in defense of the First Amendment. Just six days later, on June 28, 2002, with little fanfare, Maher's last broadcast of *PI* appeared, nearly nine years after its start on Comedy Central, with frequent guests Arianna Huffington, Christopher Reid, Ann Coulter, and Michelle Phillips. Maher then spent the remainder of the year writing *When You Ride ALONE, You Ride with Bin Laden* (2003) in response to what he saw as the government's failure to involve the American people in shared sacrifice or growth, as it did during World Wars I and II. And though without quite the national forum (or audience) he had on ABC, Maher returned to television in 2003 with a similarly themed weekly show on the pay cable channel Home Box Office titled *Real Time with Bill Maher.*

Conclusion

It is amazing that a comment made on a program known and promoted for being politically incorrect would eventually be canceled for living up to its reputation, but that scenario is precisely what occurred with *Politically Incorrect with Bill Maher.* The line the host crossed was not one that was seen by his guests, his studio audience, or his viewers but one perceived by those individuals outside the network who no longer wanted Maher to have a nationally televised forum. Maher, though not drawing the same size audience that Letterman and Leno were at the time, attracted a very upscale demographic that advertisers wanted to reach. The program's relatively low cost ensured ABC a respectable return on its investment, and the program had been on the network for five and a half years by the time of Maher's infamous remark. ABC reevaluated its position only after two main advertisers withdrew their support of the program after they were threatened with a boycott that never materialized. Rather than expose itself to a backlash, ABC chose not to force its affiliates to run *PI* while at the same time reducing or eliminating any marketing for the program on those affiliates that still ran the show. They also chose to let Maher's contract expire the following summer, skillfully deflecting the controversy back onto Maher—a "win-win" for the network, while Maher, and the American public, lost an outlet where controversial ideas were discussed on a weeknightly basis.

6 Discussion and Conclusions

This book has examined four American television programs, *The Smothers Brothers Comedy Hour, The Richard Pryor Show, TV Nation,* and *Politically Incorrect with Bill Maher,* in order to determine what led to their ultimate cancellations by looking at the background of both the political and the self-regulatory forces that have shaped American television broadcasting from 1947 to the present and how these forces impacted these programs. Additionally, the sociopolitical context of each program was examined to determine the forces at work during each program's era. Finally, a review of the content of each program—focusing on the most controversial material as defined by each program's producers, network, and audience—helped to craft the larger story for each program presented here, especially with regard to how each network directly responded to controversial content that it deemed objectionable.

Advertising, Programming, and the Networks

The "show business" that is American broadcasting provides "free" programs to the public. Revenue for networks, stations, and their respective shareholders comes from paid advertising that airs during the programs. The "business" side of this arrangement necessitates that American broadcasters provide programming that is acceptable for public viewing. The public, in exchange for this free programming, implicitly agrees to commercial interruptions that air during and between that programming. The purpose of television programs is to attract as large an audience as possible for the program's advertisers. Any given program's content must, therefore, have enough appeal to be economically viable—a complicated combination of ratings, demographics, advertising, and production costs.

Trying to please all of the concerned parties is difficult, if not impossible, because the tried-and-true formulas that networks rely on often lead to "bland television" that turns viewers away (Ferguson and Eastman 2002, 10). Networks often attempt to overcome audience disaffection with what is seen as "markedly different program ideas" (20). However, this venture can result in the broadcasting of controversial material that upsets sponsors, the general public, or government officials—and in some instances any combination of these groups.

The quiz-show scandal of the 1950s forced networks to formally sever advertisers from the creative process and sole sponsorship of commercial television programming. However, because of the symbiotic relationship between television networks and their advertisers, the fate of programs that fall on the acceptable fringes of either ratings or taste ultimately rests on their ability to ensure sufficient advertising revenue. Additional factors in the complex equation of what a network considers when retaining a controversial program include consumer boycotts (real or threatened), lawsuits (by performers or entities mentioned on a program), and a network's own willingness to rise above these issues. Networks that choose to air what is viewed as controversial material balance these items against the profitability of the program to determine a program's long-term viability.

What Was Controversial: Some Common Elements

In examining these four programs from these four networks, a common theme emerges. Network ideology strives to provide content that will not upset advertisers or the vast majority of viewers, leading to the common complaint that network television is

aimed at the lowest common denominator. When a network provides a wide latitude of freedom to content producers who have
points of view that diverge from the network's dominant ideology, it may use the opportunity to open a dialogue on controversial topics with the viewing audience. The Smothers Brothers
used their airtime to debate the merits of the Vietnam War and
the draft and embrace the countercultural movement of the late
1960s. Richard Pryor tried to discuss the issues of race and intol-
erance that persisted in the late 1970s. Michael Moore took on the
corporate machinations and political corruption of the 1990s. Bill
Maher tried to challenge blind patriotism while the United States
was still recovering from the worst terrorist attack in its history in
2001. These socially conscious producers tried to educate as well
as entertain and saw no reason they could not do both effectively.
Their respective networks strongly disagreed, claiming that these
programs did not meet network standards for broadcast. With the
passing of each program, networks reaffirmed their power base
in American culture, sending the message that diverse points of
view will be tolerated to a point and no further, and those individuals who cannot agree to these conditions will find their
shows canceled.

Why They Were Canceled

Low Ratings or Poor Scheduling?

With respect to low ratings, two of the four programs examined
fall into this category as a possible reason for their cancellations
from the network point of view. As detailed in Chapter 3, *The
Richard Pryor Show* averaged only twenty million viewers for a
third-place finish in its original time slot against the number-one
show in the country, *Happy Days*. Critics at the time claimed that
it was a poor time slot, given that it was the Family Viewing Hour,
constraining Pryor from performing the brand of humor for

which NBC presumably hired him. A smaller contributing factor to Pryor's early exit from network television may have also come in the form of a threatened boycott by homosexual groups after his infamous appearance at the Hollywood Bowl. Though the boycott never materialized, Pryor's offscreen behavior may have scared skittish network executives into giving up on his troubled production. Given the expenditure that NBC had paid to secure Pryor for the network, however, it seems that it did not do everything in its power to use his abilities for the network's benefit.

On the opposite end of the cost scale, Chapter 4 detailed the strange case of how both NBC and Fox had found a relative bargain with respect to the production of Michael Moore's *TV Nation*. With 40 percent of its production costs subsidized by the BBC, both networks could have provided more time for the program to find an audience, as both networks had done with slow starters such as *Seinfeld* and *Married . . . with Children*, respectively. The BBC scheduled the program at a later hour than its American counterparts, and it thrived in Britain while failing in the United States. Moore was hired with prior knowledge of his liberal bias and his tendency to go after the corporate executives of likely advertisers; in fact, this quality was what drew him to NBC's attention in the first place. However, it might be fair to claim—as Moore did at the time—that NBC and later Fox did not know how much of a "tempest in a teapot" they were hiring, nor did they have very much control over what topics Moore chose to pursue.

In terms of real problems faced by both networks in regards to *TV Nation,* one segment from the first season caused a legal problem that no network or affiliate wants to deal with: a libel lawsuit. Although the producers of *TV Nation* were successfully sued in Texas, the verdict was later overturned on appeal. Nonetheless, such a lawsuit can dampen a broadcast network's enthusiasm over a controversial program that garners a small niche audience, no matter how cheap it is to produce.

In retrospect, both *The Richard Pryor Show* and *TV Nation* were victims of poor network scheduling, and it could be argued that had they been properly handled, they could both have become moderate hits. Both programs suffered from network notes, meddling, and censorship, creating hostile environments for each program's production talent. Because of the stifling—or, in the case of *The Richard Pryor Show*, crippling—atmosphere found at the networks, the end result is that both programs suffered from shortened production runs.

They Crossed an "Unseen Line"?

Contrast the experiences of *The Richard Pryor Show* and *TV Nation* with the tribulations of *The Smothers Brothers Comedy Hour* and *Politically Incorrect with Bill Maher*. Both latter programs enjoyed relatively long (and profitable) production runs that were eventually cut short over issues of taste. As shown in Chapter 2, even though *The Smothers Brothers Comedy Hour* experienced a drop in ratings by its third season, it was still earning respectable ratings and had presold most of its available advertising for the 1969–1970 season when the brothers were abruptly fired. Even though the variety-show format was costly, the show was profitable, and, as discussed, the drop in ratings cannot be seen as the most viable reason for the show's termination. The Smothers Brothers' termination had more to do with differences in taste between the producers and network executives as well as the network providing a "good-faith" sacrificial lamb to silence congressional critics who were preparing new legislation to regulate controversial material on broadcast television. These points were highlighted in the Smothers Brothers' successful breach-of-contract lawsuit they brought against CBS for the loss of revenue from the "canceled" 1969–1970 season.

Likewise, *Politically Incorrect with Bill Maher* had enjoyed early phenomenal success at Comedy Central before moving to ABC.

Placed in the post-*Nightline* time slot, *Politically Incorrect* posted respectable third-place ratings while playing to a more upscale demographic than either *The Late Show with David Letterman* or *The Tonight Show*. With ABC's lowered expectations, Maher did not garner the kind of money reserved for his competitors, but since his program was relatively cheap to produce, he garnered enough money to ensure moderate profitability. Of course, the program's profitability was before the proposed boycotts of its two major sponsors forced the network to market the program at what were described as bargain rates, which were not disclosed (Carter 2001). Before Maher's comments, *PI* had been earning twenty-five thousand dollars for a thirty-second spot (Lazare 2001).

Although it may be commendable that ABC stuck by Bill Maher after his post-9/11 comments, it is evident that the network did little to market the program after the loss of sponsorship, ultimately replacing him with Jimmy Kimmel of *The Man Show* fame. It is also likely that ABC may have just let Maher's contract run out in order to avoid looking like an institutional censor, especially after he became a symbol for First Amendment activists.

In comparing the content and outcomes of *The Smothers Brothers Comedy Hour* and *Politically Incorrect with Bill Maher,* their similar fates is clearly understood. When the Smothers Brothers, as skilled satirists, began to target Nixon in their last season, they brought out the ire of newly installed CBS president Robert Wood, a Nixon supporter who did not appreciate the brothers' views. When Maher drew the wrath of the Bush administration over his post-9/11 comments, some ABC affiliates kept the program off the air, and network executives began to look quietly for Maher's replacement.

The similarity between the political deaths of these two programs was not lost on two of the principals involved. When Bill Maher was given the First Amendment Award at the U.S. Comedy

Arts Festival in March 2002, Tommy Smothers, a frequent *PI* guest, was on hand to discuss the nature of dissent in the post-9/11 world with Maher:

> SMOTHERS: When there's disagreement in national dialogues taking place in the country, when there's different points of view, criticism is very important—and so is comedy. When you're trying to share a truth that contradicts people's beliefs, it's far easier to do it in a joke. It's a softer way of teaching and giving new and different viewpoints.
>
> MAHER: It may not be easy to listen to, but that doesn't make it any less important. The Smothers Brothers, their main point, the one that got them kicked off the air essentially, was that the Vietnam War was a horrible waste, and that [was] not the conventional wisdom. . . . So apparently, they were right, but they were just ahead of everyone. (Kleiner 2002, 39)

Perhaps *South Park* executive producer and cocreator Matt Stone, also in attendance at the festival (and no stranger to controversy), put it most succinctly: "Censorship absolutely does exist, but it's not a government censor" (Gunther 2002, 36). It is the networks, through their desire to appease advertisers, that wield the power of what is seen on American television.

Although at first glance this self-censorship seems like an economic issue, advertisers may recognize that controversial programming tends to polarize audiences. If a controversial program's audience associates the advertising with an endorsement of the points of view espoused on the program, then advertisers may begin to worry, which often culminates in the withdrawal of advertising sponsorship. It is through the possible fear of negative association that the economics of network television advertising are linked with the controversial content of entertainment programming.

The Effectiveness of Viewer Protests?

The examination of these programs has also shown that a highly charged vocal minority of American broadcast television viewers can have a significant impact on television networks and their advertisers. Whether they are viewed as important business leaders, such as "supermarket crusader" Laurence A. Johnson in the 1950s (who led the fight against supposed Communists), or housewives, like Terry Rakolta (who initially convinced timid sponsors to drop *Married . . . with Children*), networks and their advertisers take the threat of boycotts and bad publicity very seriously.

It is evident that network programmers would, absent "good" fan mail, prefer to determine a program's approval or disapproval in the form of ratings, not angry letters or phone calls. Just as one ratings point represents one million viewers, networks and advertisers similarly view negative feedback from a few as just as proportionately representative. In the case of Bill Maher, Sears and Federal Express based their decisions to pull their advertising on the listeners of a conservative radio talk-show host who followed through on his advice, contacted these prominent sponsors, and made their disapproval known.

Conclusion

As previously discussed, the responsibility for what is ultimately broadcast to the American public rests, by law, with each network. Because of this obligation, American broadcast networks have every right and responsibility to enforce strict standards with regards to truly indecent material as defined by the FCC and the courts (such as foul language, explicit sexual situations, and so on)—and this duty is not in question here. However, networks also have a responsibility for helping to shape national culture with regards to the ideas they choose to broadcast, and it is on this point that their use of corporate censorship threatens American culture's diversity.

To that end, I believe that these programs represent a mere handful of socially conscious programming that producers have been permitted to deliver. In perspective, these marginalized messages were produced with a genuine desire to speak to a broader audience to both entertain and educate while under ever increasing scrutiny from network executives. On a case-by-case basis, the incidents of network censorship that each program experienced appear as isolated events set against the broader stage of American broadcasting. Collectively, however, these examples form a broader, macrolevel look at how American broadcast programming is manipulated to obtain the widest audience possible. Advertisers and network executives often censor and systematically suppress dissent in the name of protecting the public, the government, corporations, or themselves, but more often than not they do so to maintain their sources of revenue. In short, the censorship of controversial programming material maintains the status quo. Given the broadcast industry's penchant for consolidation and conglomeration with the cable industry, coupled with the symbiotic relationship that broadcasters have with advertisers, programs with points of view that threaten, frighten, or challenge that status quo seem unlikely to be aired on broadcast television or cable networks. American television networks use their censors to enforce their subjective "standards" to promote their ideology, and if a producer continues to push or stretch those standards, networks have the final say with the ultimate form of censorship: cancellation.

Works Cited

Index

Works Cited

Adair, Bill. 2005. "The Messenger vs. the Media." *St. Petersburg Times Online*, Mar. 13. http://www.sptimes.com/2005/03/13/Worldandnation/The_messenger_vs_the_.shtml.

Adalian, Josef. 1994. "'TV Nation' Is Left-Wing Fun Crafted for Everyone." *Washington Times*, July 19, C15.

Alter, Jonathan. 2001. "The Media's 'Balancing' Act." *Newsweek*, Oct. 8, 60.

Alterman, Eric. 2001. "Patriot Games." *Nation* 273, no. 13 (Oct. 29): 10.

"American Dissenters Feel the Backlash." 2001. *New Zealand Herald Online*, Sept. 28.

Armstrong, Mark. 2001a. "Maher Causes 'Cowardly' Flap." E!Online, Sept. 20. Page discontinued.

———. 2001b. "White House Politically Corrects Maher." E!Online, Sept. 27. Page discontinued.

Associated Press. 1994. "Filmmaker Michael Moore Pursues Another Auto Exec." July 12.

"At Last, Mississippi Votes to End Slavery." 1995. *Miami Herald*, Mar. 17, A1.

Barnouw, Eric. 1990. *Tube of Plenty: The Evolution of American Television*. 2d ed. New York: Oxford Univ. Press.

Belcher, Walt. 1995. "Fox Plugs into the Offbeat 'TV Nation.'" *Tampa Tribune*, July 15, Florida Television, 6.

Bessie, Alvah. 1965. *Inquisition in Eden*. East Berlin: Seven Seas Publishers.

Biddle, Frederic M. 1995. "Filmmaker Talks about TV Interview." *Boston Globe*, Jan. 16, Living, 45.

Boehlert, Eric. 2005. "Fake News, Fake Reporters." *Salon*, Feb. 10. http://dir.salon.com/story/news/feature/2005/02/10/gannon_affair/index_np.html.

Bogart, Leo. 1995. *Commercial Culture: Media Systems and the Public Interest.* New York: Oxford Univ. Press.

Brennan, Patricia. 1994. "Michael Moore: At Large." *Washington Post*, July 17, Y7.

Brooks, Tim. 1987. *The Complete Directory to Prime Time TV Stars, 1946–Present.* New York: Random House.

Brooks, Tim, and Earle Marsh. 1999. *The Complete Directory to Prime Time Network and Cable TV Shows, 1946–Present.* New York: Ballantine Books.

Brown, J. 1977. "NBC 'Stifling My Creativity.'" *Los Angeles Times*, Sept. 14, 18.

Carter, Bill. 2001. "TV Notes: Sponsors Defect." *New York Times*, Sept. 26, E7.

Carter, Bill, and Felicity Barringer. 2001. "A Nation Challenged: Speech and Expression; In Patriotic Time, Dissent Is Muted." *New York Times*, Sept. 28, A1.

Castaneda, J. C. 1995. "State's Symbolic Move: Slavery Abolishment." *USA Today*, Feb. 17, A10.

Clements, Michael. 1994. "Ford Boss Passes Filmmaker's Slick Test." *USA Today*, July 13, B1.

Coffey, D. 1990. "African American Personnel in U.S. Forces in Vietnam." In *Encyclopedia of the Vietnam War: A Political, Social, and Military History*, edited by Spencer C. Tucker. 2 vols. Santa Barbara, Calif.: ABC-Clio.

The Commission on Freedom of the Press. 1947. *A Free and Responsible Press.* Chicago: Univ. of Chicago Press.

Comstock, George, Eli Rubinstein, and John Murray, eds. 1972. *Television and Social Behavior: A Technical Report to the Surgeon General's*

Scientific Advisory Committee on Television and Social Behavior. Washington, D.C.: U.S. Government Printing Office.

Cooper, T. 2001. "2 Stations Yank 'Politically Incorrect.'" *Omaha World Herald,* Sept. 22, B8.

Cowan, Geoffrey. 1978. *See No Evil: The Backstage Battle over Sex and Violence on Television.* New York: Simon and Schuster.

Cuprisin, Tim. 2001. "Some Commentators on Attacks Cross the Line of Poor Taste." *Milwaukee Journal Sentinel,* Sept. 20, B6.

Dallos, Robert E. 1967. "Pete Seeger Gets New Chance on TV." *New York Times,* Aug. 25, 72.

Daly, Steven. 2003. "Blue Streak." *TV Guide,* Aug. 2, 28–34.

Drinkard, J. 1994. "TV Episode Takes an Irreverent Look at Lobbying in Washington." Associated Press, Aug. 1.

Dubose, Louis. 1996. "Sludge, Lies, and Videotape: When Michael Moore Whiffed N.Y. Biosolids in Texas, Should He Have Smelled Libel?" *Nation* 262 (Apr. 22): 21–22.

Dunlop, Donald. 1975. "Popular Culture and Methodology." *Journal of Popular Culture* 9: 375–83.

Fallows, James. 2003. "The Age of Murdoch." *Atlantic Monthly* (Sept.): 81–98.

Farhi, Paul. 2001. "WJLA's Correction: Pull Maher." *Washington Post,* Sept. 22, C7.

Federal Communications Commission. 1974. "Children's Television Programs: Report and Policy Statement." *Federal Register* 39 (Nov. 6): 39396–409.

Ferguson, Douglas A., and Susan T. Eastman. 2002. "A Framework for Programming Strategies." In *Broadcast/Cable/Web Programming: Strategies and Practices,* edited by Susan T. Eastman and Douglas A. Ferguson, 3–34. 6th ed. Stamford, Conn.: Wadsworth/Thompson Learning.

"Free Speech in Wartime." 2001. *Washington Post,* Sept. 29, A26.

Friend, Tom. 2001. "You Can't Say That: The Networks Play Word Games." *New Yorker,* Nov. 19, 44–49.

Friendly, Fred. 1967. *Due to Circumstances Beyond Our Control . . .* New York: Vintage.

Goldberg, Robert. 1994. "Television: Voice of the Underdog; Imported Laughs." *Wall Street Journal,* July 18, A10.

Goodson, Mark. 1991. "If I'd Stood Up Earlier." *New York Times Magazine,* Jan. 13, 22, 39–40, 43.

Gould, Jack. 1969. "TV: An Hour of Smothers." *New York Times,* Apr. 8, 95.

Gunther, Marc. 2002. "Is Free Speech a Laughing Matter?" *Fortune,* Mar. 18, 36.

Haskins, Jim. 1984. *Richard Pryor: A Man and His Madness.* New York: Beaufort Books.

Heinke, Rex S., and Michelle H. Tremain. 2000. "Influencing Media Content Through the Legal System: A Less than Perfect Solution for Advocacy Groups." In *Advocacy Groups and the Entertainment Industry,* edited by Michael Suman and Gabriel Rossman, 43–52. Westport, Conn.: Praeger.

Helm, Richard. 1995. "One More Time: Film-maker Michael Moore Turns His Acerbic Wit to Another Summer of *TV Nation.*" *Calgary Herald,* July 16, E4.

Hentoff, Nat. 1969. "The Smothers Brothers: Who Controls TV?" *Look,* June 24, 27–29.

Holloway, Dianne. 2002. "'Politically Incorrect' Died Before Sept. 11 Furor." *Cox News Service,* June 27, D4.

Hoyt, Olga C., and Edwin P. Hoyt. 1970. *Censorship in America.* New York: Seabury Press.

Johnson, Nicholas. 1970. *How to Talk Back to Your Television Set.* Boston: Little, Brown.

Keveney, Bill. 2001. "Late-Night TV Shows Return, Toned Down." *USA Today,* Sept. 18, C12.

Kirn, Walter. 2002. "The End of the Affair." *New York Times Magazine,* May 26, 11–12.

Kisner, Ronald E. 1977. "Pryor Adds to Fireworks to Star-Spangled 'Gay Night.'" *Jet,* Oct. 6, 55–56.

Kleiner, Carolyn. 2002. "What's So Funny?" *U.S. News and World Report,* Mar. 25, 39.

Kloman, William. 1969. "The Transmogrification of the Smothers Brothers." *Esquire,* Oct., 149.

Lazare, Lewis. 2001. "Sears Pulls 'Incorrect' Ads." *Chicago Sun-Times,* Sept. 20, 7.

Leab, Daniel J. 1970. "Response to the Hutchins Commission." *Gazette* 16, no. 2: 105–13.

Leiser, Ken. 2007. "Doe Run Ordered to Clean Up Its Act." *St. Louis Post-Dispatch,* Mar. 21. http://www.stltoday/stltoday news/stories. nsf/stlouiscitycounty/story/0748A64060844C1E862572A5001317 1D?OpenDocument.

Lelyveld, Joseph. 1977. "Off Color." *New York Times Magazine,* Nov. 6, 174.

Leonard, J. 1969. "A Question of Taste—or Is It?" *Life,* May 16, 24.

Levin, David P. 1994. "Tweaking the Captains of Industry in Prime Time." *New York Times,* July 13, D1.

Lewis, Justin. 1999. "Reproducing Political Consent in the United States." *Critical Studies in Mass Communication* 16: 251–67.

Lewis, Richard W. 1969. "St. Thomas and the Dragon." *Playboy,* Aug., 141, 179–91.

Lipsitz, George. 1988. "'This Ain't No Sideshow': Historians and Media Studies." *Critical Studies in Mass Communication* 5: 147–61.

Loynd, Roy. 1994. "TV Nation." *Variety,* July 19, 25.

Lucas, Scott. 2001. "How a Free Press Censors Itself." *New Statesman* 130, no. 4563 (Nov. 12): 14–15.

MacCarthy, M. M. 1995. "Broadcast Self-regulation: The NAB, Codes, Family Viewing Hour, and Television Violence." *Cardozza Arts and Entertainment* 13: 667–96.

Maher, Bill. 2003. *When You Ride* ALONE, *You Ride with Bin Laden.* Beverly Hills: New Millennium Press.

McNeil, Alex. 1991. *Total Television: A Comprehensive Guide to Programming from 1948 to the Present.* 3d ed. New York: Penguin.

Metz, Robert. 1975. *CBS: Reflections in a Bloodshot Eye.* New York: Signet.

Mifflin, Lawrie. 1995. "The Rib Tickler's Approach to Social Provocation." *New York Times,* July 16, sec. 2, 24.

Moore, Frazier. 1994. "Michael Moore's Revenge: The Hilarious 'TV Nation.'" Associated Press, July 15.

Moore, Michael, and Kathleen Glynn. 1998. *Adventures in a TV Nation.* New York: Harper Perennial.

Murray, Matthew J. 1997. "Broadcast Content Regulation and Cultural Limits, 1920–1962." Ph.D. diss., Univ. of Wisconsin–Madison.

National Urban League. 1977. "The State of Black America, 1977." *Black Scholar* (Sept.): 2–8.

Navasky, Victor S. 1980. *Naming Names.* New York: Penguin.

""A New Black Superstar." 1977. *Time,* Aug. 22, 66–67.

Nichols, Nichelle. 1994. *Beyond Uhura.* New York: G. P. Putnam's Sons.

O'Connor, John J. 1977. "TV: Pryor's Art Is Strong Stuff—'Soap' Weak." *New York Times,* Sept. 13, 62.

———. 1994. "New Targets Lined Up for a Deadpan Deadeye." *New York Times,* July 19, C15.

Orth, Maureen. 1977. "The Perils of Pryor." *Newsweek,* Oct. 3, 60.

Papazian, Ed. 1989. *Medium Rare: The Evolution, Workings, and Impact of Commercial Television.* New York: Media Dynamics, 1989.

"Plaintiffs Win Venue Change." 2004. *Columbia (Mo.) Daily Tribune,* Feb. 11, A12.

"Politically Incorrect and Protected." 2001. *St. Petersburg Times,* Sept. 30, D2.

Pryor, Richard. 1995. *Pryor Convictions and Other Life Sentences.* New York: Pantheon Books.

"A Pryor Restraint: Out Goes the First Minute of the First Show." 1977. *Washington Post,* Sept. 14, B1.

Quill, Greg. 1995. "Hilariously Subversive Moore Is Coming Back." *Toronto Star,* July 14, B11.

Reilly, S. 1978. "Life Is No Laughing Matter for America's Blackest Comic and Movie Star—Richard Pryor." *People,* Mar. 13, 44–49.

Robbins, J. Max. 1995. "Moore Wanted More NBC." *Variety,* Feb. 6, Television, 25.

Robinson, Louis. 1978. "Richard Pryor Talks . . . about Love, Life, Humor, Marriage—and What Happened to His Television Show." *Ebony,* Jan., 116–22.

Rothenberg, Randall. 2001. "For Country in Need of Laugh, Joke Ends Up Being on Maher." *Advertising Age* 72, no. 41 (Oct. 8): 21.

Rovin, Jeff. 1984. *Richard Pryor: Black and Blue.* New York: Bantam Books.

Ryan, James. 1994. "Michael Moore Takes Satirical Wit on the Road." BPI Entertainment News Wire, July 8.

Ryan, Joal. 1998. "The P.C. Police vs. Bill Maher." E!Online, Oct. 29. Page discontinued.

Schlussel, Debbie. 2001. "Bill Maher Was Right." WorldNetDaily, Sept. 21. http://www.worldnetdaily.com/news/article.asp?ARTICLE _ID=24606.

Schneider, Alfred R., with Kaye Pullen. 2001. *The Gatekeeper: My 30 Years as a TV Censor.* Syracuse: Syracuse Univ. Press.

Seeger, Pete. 1967. *"Waist Deep in the Big Muddy," and Other Love Songs.* Columbia CL 2705/CS 9505.

Selnow, Gary W., and Richard R. Gilbert. 1993. *Society's Impact on Television: How the Viewing Public Shapes Television Programming.* Westport, Conn.: Praeger.

Shales, Tom. 1977. "The New Season: Pryor's Angry Humor, the Savagery of *Soap.*" *Washington Post,* Sept. 13, B1.

———. 1995. "Michael Moore: Return of a Prank Amateur." *Washington Post,* July 21, C1.

Smothers, Tom. 1969. "Are the Brothers Being Smothered?" *New York Times,* June 29, 27.

Spector, Bert. 1983. "A Class of Cultures: The Smothers Brothers vs. CBS Television." In *American History/American Television: Interpreting the Video Past,* edited by John E. O'Connor. New York: Frederick Unger Publishing.

Stauber, John, and Sheldon Rampton. 1995. *Toxic Sludge Is Good for You: Lies, Damn Lies, and the Public Relations Industry.* Monroe, Maine: Common Courage Press.

Stone, Judy. 1969. "Two Clean-Cut Heroes Make Waves." *New York Times,* Apr. 16, sec. 2, 21.

"TV-Industry View on Speech Scored." 1969. *New York Times,* Apr. 9.

U.S. Bureau of the Census. 1999. "Resident Population Characteristics [Race and Sex] Percent Distribution and Median Age, 1850–1998, and Projections, 2000 to 2050." In *Statistical Abstract of the U.S.* Washington, D.C.: U.S. Bureau of the Census.

U.S. Senate. Committee on the Judiciary. Subcommittee to Investigate Juvenile Delinquency. 1962. "Juvenile Delinquency." File, Jan. 24. Washington, D.C.: Government Printing Office.

Vaughn, Robert. 1972. *Only Victims: A Study of Show Business Blacklisting.* New York: G. P. Putnam's Sons.

Vilbig, Peter. 2001. "Arrested Liberties?" *New York Times Upfront* 134, no. 5 (Nov. 12): 10–15.

Walter, Tom. 1995. "White Slaves Hilariously Mirror Nation's Tragedy." *Memphis Commercial Appeal,* July 15, C1.

Ward, Scott, Greg Reale, and David Levinson. 1972. "Children's Perceptions, Explanations, and Judgments of Television Advertising: A Further Exploration." In *Television and Social Behavior: A Technical Report to the Surgeon General's Scientific Advisory Committee on Television and Social Behavior,* edited by George Comstock, E. Rubinstein, and J. Murray, 468–90. Washington, D.C.: U.S. Government Printing Office.

Weiseltier, Leon. 2001. "Heroes." *New Republic* 225, no. 16 (Oct. 15): 66.

Werner, James D. 2003. "RE: April 1, 2003, Draft Lead Transportation and Materials Handling Plan, Herculaneum, Missouri." Missouri

Department of Natural Resources, Apr. 4. http://www.dnr.mo.gov/env/DR4-4-03.pdf.

Wershba, Joseph. 2000. "Edward R. Murrow and the Man of His Time." *Eve's Magazine.* http://www.evesmag.com/Murrow.htm.

"What's Acceptable to Say in the Wake of the Terrorist Attacks." 2001. *Marketplace,* Sept. 27. http://learcenter.org/pdf/mp092701.pdf.

White House. 2001. "Press Briefing by Ari Fleischer." Topic 18, Sept. 26. http://www.whitehouse.gov/news/releases/2001/09/20010926-5.html.

Whitney, Dwight. 1968. "Irreverent Is Word for the Smothers Brothers." *TV Guide,* Feb. 10, 15–19.

Wickham, DeWayne. 2001. "Pulling Ads Off Maher's TV Show Is 'Cowardly.'" *USA Today Online,* Oct. 12. http://www.usatoday.com/news/opinion/columnists/wickham/2001-09-21-wickham.htm.

Williams, John A., and Dennis A. Williams. 1991. *If I Stop I'll Die: The Comedy and Tragedy of Richard Pryor.* New York: Thunder's Mouth Press.

Index

ABC (American Broadcasting
Company): acquisition of, 28,
100; *Bus Stop,* 14–15; *Ellen,* 133;
as established radio network,
6; *Happy Days,* 62, 72, 92, 93,
148; *Laverne & Shirley,* 72, 92, 93;
The Name's the Same, 9; negative
stories about Disney killed by,
100; and Pastore plan for NAB
prescreening, 16; on reducing advertising in children's
television, 18; *Roots,* 1, 79, 79n,
87, 93; Standards and Practices
Department eliminated by, 24.
*See also Politically Incorrect with
Bill Maher*
abortion protestors, 115–17, 125,
126
Action for Children's Television
(ACT), 18, 19
Adalian, Josef, 104
Administrative Procedure Act, 20
Adventures in a TV Nation (Moore
and Glynn), 100
Adventures of Ozzie & Harriet, 13
advertisers. *See* sponsors
(advertisers)
Advertising Age, 142–43

African Americans: National Ur-
ban League's "The State of Black
America," 67; programming
written by whites, 67, 79; in *The
Richard Pryor Show*'s "Egypt,
1909" skit, 78–79; in *The Richard
Pryor Show*'s "The First Black
President of the United States"
skit, 66–71; in *The Richard Pryor
Show*'s "The Mississippi Rape
Trial" skit, 72–78; in *The Richard
Pryor Show*'s "*Titanic* Lifeboat"
skit, 87–88; in *The Smothers
Brothers Comedy Hour* skit on
the draft, 47; in *TV Nation*'s
"Love Night" segment, 124;
TV Nation's reenactment of Los
Angeles riots, 121
Alda, Alan, 103
All in the Family, 1, 19, 33, 53
Allison, Alegra, 85
American Broadcasting Company.
See ABC (American Broadcast-
ing Company)
American Business Consultants, 8
American Civil Liberties Union, 7
Andy Griffith Show, The, 34
Annenberg, Walter, 51

Carter, Jimmy, 70, 85

CBS (Columbia Broadcasting System): on ABC plan to reduce advertising in children's television, 18; acquisition of, 28–29; *All in the Family,* 1, 19, 33, 53; *The Ed Sullivan Show,* 46, 56, 64, 65; as established radio network, 6; Family Viewing Hour of, 19, 20; kills story about tobacco industry, 100; *Late Night with David Letterman,* 102, 144, 151; *M*A*S*H,* 19, 33; Jackie Mason lawsuit against, 55–56; as media conglomerate, 29; and Pastore plan for NAB prescreening, 16–17; prescreening of programs by, 49, 58; *See It Now,* 10–12; *60 Minutes,* 84n. 11, 100, 101, 103, 104; Smothers Brothers' breach-of-contract lawsuit against, 53, 59, 150; Standards and Practices Department reduced by, 24; standard 1960s family fare of, 34; traditional guest stars of, 36. *See also Smothers Brothers Comedy Hour, The;* Stanton, Frank

"Censor, The" (Williams), 53–54

censorship. *See* television censorship

Chambers, Ernest, 38

Chasey, Bill, 107–8

Cheyenne, 13

children: censorship of *The Richard Pryor Show* for protection of, 65; Children's Television Act of 1990, 22, 25–26; deregulation of

children's programming, 21–22; FCC concern about television content for, 17–19, 25–26; ratings system for protection of, 26–27; V-chip for protection of, 26, 27

"Children's Perceptions, Expectations, and Judgments of Television Advertising: A Further Exploration" (Ward, Reale, and Levinson), 18

Children's Television Act (1990), 22, 25–26

"Children's Television Programs: Report and Policy Statement" (Federal Communications Commission), 18

Cleaver, Jim, 96

Clinton, Bill, 26, 135

CNN, 29

Cobb County, Georgia, 121–23

Coble, Howard, 108

Columbia Broadcasting System. *See* CBS (Columbia Broadcasting System)

Columbia TriStar, 109, 118, 123, 129

Comedy Central, 132, 150

Commission on Freedom of the Press (Hutchins Commission), 4–5, 6, 35

Committee, the, 43, 43n. 14

Communications Act (1934), 6

competition, Telecommunications Act of 1996 said to enhance, 26, 28

condoms, 114–15

Cook, Fred, 22–23

cop shows, 13

Corey, Jeff, 62, 74